NEVER

LESSONS LEARNED FROM FORTY-FIVE YEARS
OF RUNNING WITHOUT MISSING A DAY

MISSED

MARK COVERT

WITH CHRIS COVERT

Cover image by: Scott Schweitzer

ISBN: 978-1-7323362-4-7

Edited by: Amy Ashby

Warren
publishing

Published by Warren Publishing
Charlotte, NC
www.warrenpublishing.net
Printed in the United States

ACKNOWLEDGMENTS
MARK COVERT

'd first like to thank my oldest son, Chris, who took this project on and saw it through to the end. He has spent unknown hours researching, interviewing people, and listening to me tell stories repeatedly. I can't thank him enough.

When I was growing up, I was lucky to have two of the greatest parents in the world. Just like all kids, there were times when they would make me so mad, I didn't know what to say to them, but in the end, they were always there for me. My dad was a tough guy. He joined the Marines during WWII and was a Purple Heart recipient. He changed through the years, but he stayed very much the same. My mom was a stay-at-home mom who took her job just as seriously as my dad took being in the Marines. She ran the house. She made breakfast, our lunches, did the laundry, had dinner on the table, and was always there when we needed her. It was her house and she ran it her way, but she always knew what my brother and I needed. Between the two of them, my brother and I were always encouraged to try new things and never be afraid of trying to be the best.

The limited amount of success I had as a runner and coach was due to two people, Frank Kallem and Laszlo Tabori. Kallem got me started at Burbank High. Always encouraging, but always challenging, he was the biggest reason why my streak started. In just two years, Tabori took me from a very average high school distance runner to someone who could dream of making an Olympic team. He was a hard ass, tough guy, coaching someone who was very much like him. I can't thank him enough for making me the runner and coach I became.

But the biggest thank you of all goes to my wife, Debi, and my four children, Chris, Brittany, Patrick, and Ashley. When Debi came into my life, my life changed forever. She is my biggest supporter in every way. Always understanding when I would go on a run, staying with a coach's life for all these years. Morning practices, vacations, always working around the cross country and track seasons. Often her only trips were when she would go with me out of town when I was recruiting. All this while we were raising four children. She is and always will be the one and only love of my life. As for my children, they were born into something I don't think they thought would ever end. The Streak and my coaching were a part of their life. They didn't know anything else. My kids can all run Hy-Tek along with my wife and two of them can run the FinishLynx system. Our children have all grown up and gone their own ways, but they, along with Debi, were the reason I kept going to work every day. When you have a family that is so special, you don't want to let them down.

Finally, to all the students, athletes, family, and friends who passed through The Streak. Thank you for always being so supportive in this part of my life. For those who were on my teams, thank you for believing in me. We had a lot of fun along the way. You are the ones who will tell the stories of our summer training camps, the workouts, and the meets. The stories seem to only get better as the years go on, but because of all of you, there are stories to tell.

I hope you enjoy the book.

—*Mark Covert*

ACKNOWLEDGMENTS
CHRIS COVERT

First, I want to thank my dad for allowing me to be a part of this project and telling his story. I was able to learn more about him and the history of my family than I ever had imagined because of it. Thank you for your continued support and mentorship in all my endeavors. To my mother for her constant support of this project and throughout my life. To my brother, sisters, and their spouses, along with my grandparents, aunts, and uncles. Even if we spoke about this book infrequently, your influence and support was always felt.

A very great "thank you" goes to the Warren Publishing team for the continued excitement and professionalism the team showed during this process. Also, to Patricia Presinary and the Archives and Special Collections Department at California State University, Fullerton.

To everyone who took the time to be interviewed and contribute: Steve Brumwell, Craig Carson, Daniel Cobian, Jackie Hansen, Jean Harvey, Andy Ligietti, Bobby Thomas, and Dave White.

Thank you to all of those who have assisted in guiding me on my professional journey as a coach, consultant, operative, and now a writer. Especially Brady Quirk-Garvin, Richard Hricik, Jack Maloney, Jack O'Toole, Phil Noble, Wilton Wright, Bill Sutherland. I especially want to thank

Dr. Ken Ravizza, whose passing near the completion of this book was difficult to bear, but memory and lessons about sports and life provide internal strength not just to myself, but to so many of us who called him teacher and friend.

To those whose friendship influenced so many of the words that were written in this project: Alex Askew, Julia Barnes, Kass Bessert, Robert Becker, Ernest Boston, Matt Pegler, James Chersonsky, Marc Davis, Jay Jones, Kevin Lasure, Anna Lefitz, Christale Spain, Paul Stovall, Peter Tecklenburg, and Spencer Toth.

To my second family, whose friendship not only provided me with much-needed breaks from work with ridiculous amounts of humor and great friendship, but acted as a compass for this project in all of its stages: Kat & Dan Beckman, John & Ashley Sousa, David Huyssen & Mary Reynolds, Kim Bowlin & Dan Ryan, Kate and Michael Hauenstein, Angela & Jonathan Hudson, Honor Sachs, and Tammy Ingram.

To my sons Jordan and Adam. Each day your knowledge, wit, and amazing smiles provide me with a joy that can't be described in any book. Nothing I have achieved, or ever will accomplish, tops the pride I feel in being able to be your dad. I so look forward to seeing everything you both will do and witnessing the great men you will become.

Lastly, to my best friend and wife, Lisa. One of the reasons I wanted to be a part of this work was to be able to write about how grateful and thankful I am for your friendship, love, and patience. Some people wait far too long for someone to enter into their life who understands them in a way that makes them feel as if they are never alone, so that in times of struggle, they have a person to turn to and discuss what lies on their heart. Someone who is not just a partner, but a teammate. I consider myself so very lucky to have this person in you. And if the struggles of life become so hard to bear that I feel there is no end in sight to its darkness, knowing you will be there is the comfort I know will provide hope in another day. My hope is that I can be the same to you and it is, and always will be, the focus of everything I do.

—*Chris Covert*

TABLE OF CONTENTS

The average person will cover
110,000 miles in their lifetime.

During his forty-five-year running streak,
Mark Covert covered over 159,000 miles.
...Enough to circle the earth
seven-and-a-half times.

FOREWORD

At 6 a.m. on July 24, 2013, in Lancaster, California, a desert town located seventy miles northeast of Downtown Los Angeles, it was seventy-five degrees with a slight breeze. While cars were already filling the streets, most of them heading to the 14 Freeway to begin their daily commute, my cross country team, the Antelope Valley College Marauders, met for our morning practice. It was the same time that practice had started for me since 1970.

What made this morning unique compared to other practices was that it was the first morning in forty-five years that I didn't go on a run.

The previous day, my family, friends, former athletes, teammates, and supporters from across the country had gathered at Antelope Valley College, the place where I had coached for over twenty years, for the last in a series of runs that had lasted for nearly half a century.

Over the past forty-five years, I had run in over 500 locations—places like Phoenix, Arizona, and New Haven, Connecticut; Tokyo, Japan, and Charleston, South Carolina. Enough miles were run during The Streak (over 159,000 during The Streak and over 163,000 overall) to circle the circumference of the earth seven-and-a-half times, the same distance as traveling from Maine to Hawaii thirty-one times, or roughly sixty percent of a trip to the moon. My journey had taken me from an average high school runner with plans to become a junior varsity football place kicker, to a collegiate national cross country champion, to competing in the 1972 Olympic Trials in the first Nike shoe to cross a finish line. I had coached state champions, national champions, world champions, and worked with enough conference champions to fill several busloads of athletes.

The Streak lasted the terms of nine different US Presidents and over the course of multiple wars. I ran twenty-three miles the day a man walked on the moon for the first time, nineteen miles on the day that John Lennon was shot, twelve on the day the Berlin Wall came down, and six the morning the Twin Towers fell. I got my run in during earthquakes, severe thunderstorms, and pounding hail that left cuts across my face. For forty-five years, if someone had come up to me and asked if I was still running, my answer to them was always the same: "The Streak is alive."

Until the day it wasn't. The total midfoot collapse of my right foot made it nearly impossible for me to run without falling and just as hard to get up out of a chair. Over the span of The Streak, doctors concluded that I had at least seven stress fractures and had torn my Achilles tendon on multiple occasions. And although The Streak continued the day after I had surgery on my meniscus, and during a stint in the hospital during a bout of kidney stones (the doctors were nice enough to let me jog around the hospital while my son held my IV bag)—I knew that things were eventually going to have to come to an end. Getting around had become so difficult that upon seeing me take my first steps for my last run, former athletes and teammates of mine surrounded me as to make sure I wouldn't fall (which had started to become a regular occurrence during those last days).

To say it was time to take a day off after forty-five years was a bit of an understatement.

When I think about those 16,436 consecutive days that I ran, I realize I got more out of The Streak than just fun memories and battered feet. Running each day taught me important lessons that shaped my approach to every aspect of my life. These were lessons about toughness I had learned from my parents, who never missed a day of work, skills I gained when I trained over 200 miles a week, and tools I used when I would get my run in each day at 4 a.m. during my career as a traveling salesman, a job that kept me on the road over 150 days a year.

When I decided I wanted to tell my story, my first thought was to write a memoir of what I had experienced over the last half-a-century. I knew I didn't want to have a ghostwriter I had never met tell my story. Instead, I wanted the help of someone I knew and trusted; someone who had an idea of what The Streak meant to me and others. Luckily, I didn't have to look very far.

My eldest son, Chris, who went for his first run with me when he was in fourth grade and who I coached while he was in junior college, graduated from California State University Fullerton (just like my youngest son, Patrick, and me), where he was the captain of the cross country team.

Chris went on to be a conference championship–winning track coach, work in national politics, and now owns a sports psychology firm, where he works with athletes, businesses, and teams across the county on mental and organizational training. After chatting with him about the book, he suggested we discuss my lessons learned and how others can apply them to their own journeys—much like he does with individuals and teams he works with. It's been a wonderful experience to work with him on this project.

This is not a book about how to train for a new personal best in the 5K or how to start a streak of your own. Rather, it is the story of *how* I got to each day in The Streak via lessons and skills learned along the way and how you can implement the same skills into your life. Here's what I hope to share with you:

- What I learned about **toughness** from my father (a Purple Heart recipient, drill instructor, and butcher) and mother (a housekeeper who loved roller derby and was just as tough as my dad);

- What I learned about **becoming the best version of myself** from my teammates and coaches while at Burbank High School (where I was at best an average runner), Los Angeles Valley College (where I became the state cross country champion), and California State University, Fullerton (where I would win a NCAA cross country individual championship and be a part of a national championship team);

- How I learned to **embrace opportunity** during the 1972 Olympic Trials in Eugene, Oregon (while wearing the first pair of Nike Waffle Racers "moon shoes");

- How I learned what **hard work** was really like as a traveling salesman on the road 150 days out of the year;
- The importance of having a **routine**—which was the same for me nearly every day for forty-five years;
- How the **relationships** with people who mattered the most continually motivated me and gave me perspective during each run;
- And how I learned **the right time to walk away.**

Throughout the pages of this book, I'll share what I learned, but I also want to provide an opportunity for you to examine your and/or your team's current journey. Each chapter will include questions designed to help you reflect on your past experiences, examine current situations, and envision scenarios that might happen down the road, so you can be prepared for wherever your journey takes you. (At the end of the book, we've compiled the questions from each chapter for you to use whenever you need them.) This book is your personal guide to discovering deeper levels of commitment and preparedness, learning when and why you should take risks, and understanding how and why you should strive to be the best version of yourself.

I didn't wake up one morning and decide I was going to run for over 16,000 days in a row. I didn't simply decide I'd run on the days my kids were born, or on the days each of my parents passed away. But The Streak taught me how to deal with each of these life events while continuing to reach for my goals, no matter how lofty they were or how challenging the obstacle was that stood in my way. Running was something I enjoyed doing each day and I made a commitment to it. I hope through reading this book you discover the one thing you love doing, make a commitment to it, and use the included lessons to help you achieve your goals.

Upon the conclusion of my final run, I said a few words to everyone who had been nice enough to be a part of that final day. One of the things I said was, "everyone who has either been on a run with me or who I have met during the span of The Streak has been instrumental to it"—which was true. And although The Streak officially began on July 23, 1968, the two most instrumental people in teaching me the skills I needed to stick with it were my mother and father. My story begins with the lessons they taught me on how to be tough.

PART I
LESSONS IN TOUGHNESS

TIME FRAME:
November 24, 1950–October 30, 1968
TOTAL DAYS RUN CONSECUTIVELY:
2 months (best at the time)
TOTAL MILES RUN: 5,000
BIGGEST MILEAGE WEEK: 81
TOTAL DISTANCE COVERED: The distance
between Anchorage, Alaska, and Miami, Florida
HISTORY:
- Korean War begins
- DNA discovered
- Vietnam War begins
- The last Civil War veteran dies at age 106
- Alaska becomes part of the USA
- Barack Obama born
- JFK assassinated
- Malcom X assassinated
- Rolling Stone Magazine founded

I did not run every day.

MY FIRST TEACHERS

What would eventually become over 16,000 days of running without taking a day off began with an education in toughness. The instructors? My mother and father. Dad, Herb Sr., was a World War II veteran and Purple Heart recipient for his service in what was one of the South Pacific's bloodiest fights, The Battle of Peleliu. Before leaving to fight, Dad had married his high school sweetheart, my mother, Elise. After being honorably discharged from the Marines, he went into the family business. Along with three of my four uncles he worked as a butcher at the local meat market in Aurora, Illinois, where both my brother Herb, Jr., and I were born.

We eventually moved to the greater Los Angeles area, settling in Burbank, which at the time was home to nearly 85,000 people. Burbank was a company town full of mostly commuters. Many veterans started families there after the war; it was a wonderful place to grow up with so many kids around the same age. Our house on Manning Street, a white, 800-square-foot post-war one-story, was located just a short bike ride from some of the best parks and playgrounds in town. That's where my parents would call home for the next forty-five years.

Being a butcher in the 1950s was very different than what you see in grocery stores today. Trucks would arrive early in the morning with big slabs of beef (like the ones Rocky beat the hell out of) and the butchers would saw, cut, slice, and wrap them up to sell. Dad would usually work six days a week, getting up at four in the morning with Mom and not arriving home until six o'clock each night. A few days a week, he would come home, have dinner, and head back out to teach meat-carving courses to butchers-in-training.

Mom stayed home and managed the house with warmth and gusto. With her in charge, everyone was up at the same time each day, their meals ready, and the house was always in working order. If we ever needed help with anything at any time, whether it was getting ready for a practice or tying bags onto our bicycles for paper routes, my mom never failed to be a source of help and comfort for me and my brother.

Dad was nothing short of a real character. He had an incredible combination of stoicism, sense of humor, and respect for others that still amazes me to this day. His thin, jet-black hair and squatty body were always accompanied by a cigar. When I was in college, one of my cross country teammates came to visit. We walked into the backyard, where Dad was grilling steaks. Upon seeing Dad's cigar dangling from his mouth and his forehead sweat dripping onto our meat, my friend exclaimed, "Holy shit—Covert's Dad is Archie Bunker!"

My mother loved to laugh as much as Dad and was a huge fan of roller derby. Although she never learned how to drive, she never missed one of my or my brother's sports competitions or school functions. And though my folks loved to laugh, tell jokes, and have a fun time, behind the smiles and hugs they were, without a shadow of a doubt, the two toughest people I have ever come across in my life.

One evening, Dad came home from work with his right hand swollen to twice its normal size and wrapped in thick bandages that were soaked in blood. It turns out that while using a butcher's saw earlier that morning, he had sliced his palm right down the middle. He told us that when he'd cut it, it looked like a raw filet of beef. He immediately left the store and drove himself to the doctor. Within a half hour, he'd been given thirty stitches and gone right back to work. As we all stood there in shock, he told us he was going to try to get some sleep so he could head into work the next day (although the tears in his eyes made me think it wasn't going to happen).

Early the next morning I overheard my parents discussing whether Dad should go into work. While Mom protested, Dad persisted. "I need to go to work," he said stubbornly. "There are shifts at the store that need to be filled. If I'm not there, we will lose money, and so will the store. We need to do whatever we can to make sure I can go in." After further debate, Dad took some pain pills the doctor had given him, and my mom put a steel mesh glove that she found in our garage (like one worn during the medieval period) over his injured hand. He kissed her good-bye and drove himself into work that morning, using his good hand to steer the car. He never took a day off from work due to that injury or any other that would happen over the next thirty-five years of his career.

Seeing how my father handled injury, along with my mother's relentless work ethic, is where I began to learn what toughness was. **I define "toughness" as the ability to do something you don't want to do, regardless of being "not in the mood," injured, or sick.** Growing up, when we had practice, we went to practice. When we had class, we went to school. This mindset of consistency traveled with me throughout my life whether I was coaching, training, or working as a salesman. There were very few excuses as to why something could not or should not get done in my house.

Whether it's at work when you want to go home after a twelve-hour shift, in athletics when you don't want to do that last repetition, or in a relationship when you need to have a conversation that may be uncomfortable, doing the thing you don't want to do can and will help you get closer to achieving your goals. It is just a matter of your drive to either be tough or settle for the way things are.

THE THREE COMPONENTS OF TOUGHNESS

I believe being tough comes from a combination of several skills. My parents taught me the first three of these skills: **commitment, preparation,** and **positive self-talk.** As much as these skills are important individually, when you blend them together, that's when you can start to tackle the tough stuff. Although each of us has different areas in which we wish to succeed, we are all able to commit to something, prepare as best we can, and communicate with ourselves in ways that can positively affect our performance. Remember, no one comes out of the womb lifting weights rather than rattles. They learn the skills that make them what they are—and yes, you can do the same.

For Dad, commitment was going into work no matter what and remembering the responsibility he had to our family as the lone breadwinner. With Dad at the store nearly all day, Mom kept the house functioning no matter what her frame of mind or how she felt. That was commitment for them—family, work, and then everything else. For you, commitment might be something different. It may be making sure you're at practice on time or putting down the cell phone at night to be fully present for your kids. As I got older, keeping my running streak going was not just about upholding the commitment I made to myself, but about showing my family and the team I was coaching the *importance* of commitment. I wanted to show them the importance of doing something you say you're going to do.

How I felt in the morning or what the weather looked like never had a bearing on whether I was going to run each day; I was always committed to improving, no matter what stage in my running career. As a coach, athletes would often come to me with some poor excuse for missing practice (it happened more than I would have liked). I always hoped witnessing me work out each day would teach them that if you are going to do something, you have to be all in, and you have to be committed all the time.

I don't believe a person can be tough without preparation. Preparation can come in the form of hours spent on the practice field or weeks spent studying for the bar exam. Dad's preparation was a routine he went through each night.

Once the house had quieted down and it was getting close to bedtime, he would walk into the kitchen and sharpen his knives. It wasn't an activity he took lightly. For nearly an hour, he would examine the sharpness of each blade and the touch of every handle. Because these knives weren't purchased over the counter at a drug store for ninety-nine cents, their preservation was foreseen with incredible care and precision. If those blades weren't ready to go when he walked into the store, Dad's ability to get work done in the manner he expected would be out the window the second he attempted to slice through a piece of meat.

Remarkable things are rarely accomplished by those who haven't put the time in to accomplish them. You may have thought cutting meat wasn't so sexy or couldn't be done in a remarkable way. But to Dad, it was. He wanted not just to do his job well, but to be great. My parents believed that in order to take part in an activity and be great at it, you had to be prepared for greatness. Those who take the time to train and read and study and learn, whether it's every day or not, have a much better chance of achieving what they set out to do than those who just show up. When the big dance comes, those who prepared are ready.

People who are great at what they do tend to get excited over the necessary things—patience, precision, and planning. Of course it's hard to be that prepared, but when done right, and with passion, these folks realize they can do it again. Then they are ready for their moment.

Toughness also involves how you speak to yourself, which is what many people refer to as "self-talk." My parents never accepted nor tolerated my brother and I feeling sorry for ourselves, or saying negative things about ourselves if something didn't work out the way we wanted. Whether we had failed a test or lost a game, not one time were we allowed to pout, mope, whine, or complain. That was considered unacceptable. We were always told we needed to not only prepare better and be more focused, but to stop, right then, with the negative self-talk. If a person of less-than-average strength or speed can become powerful and fast by training, so too can a person of weak mindedness and negative thinking become mentally strong by becoming aware of their negative internal dialogue and adjusting it.

It's crucial to speak to yourself in a positive manner. Self-defeating talk is extremely counterproductive. Confidence comes from the volume and quality of the work we do, as well as how we speak to ourselves. When was the last time you felt good about yourself while simultaneously calling yourself a piece of shit? Probably never. We all place more pressure on ourselves by creating stories in our head that are, for the most part, not true. Saying, for example, that you're going to have to drop out of school, and your parents won't speak to you anymore if you don't run well, is a story that many an athlete has told themselves before an important race. But, just like most thoughts that involve negative self-talk, something that grandiose is probably not going to happen. These stories we tell ourselves create undue pressure. The more positively you talk to yourself, the more you believe in the work you've put in, and the more you stay in the here-and-now, the less pressure you're going to feel when you need to be at your best.

CREATE YOUR OWN
DEFINITION OF "TOUGHNESS"

As important as it is to understand that toughness is doing things you don't want to do, I've also learned **it's important to create your own definition of toughness specific to the challenge you're dealing with.** Everyone has something unique they don't want to but *need* to do to be successful. Toughness for my brother was different than it was for me, as he made the decision to join the Marines right out of high school. Toughness was different for my wife, Debi, who went back to school when she was in her thirties to become a teacher, all while raising our four kids and working full-time.

For you, toughness may mean sucking it up to get ready for your conference championship, when spending time with your friends seems much more appealing. Getting out to the gym each day may be the toughest thing to do after a long day at work, when you'd rather go home to watch Netflix. Whatever your personal definition of toughness is, it needs to be just for you so you know how to prepare and communicate with yourself when things get hard. Remember, **toughness means doing something that you don't want to do.** What is that something for you and how are you going to do it anyway?

QUESTION: How do you define "toughness"?

DISCOVERING RUNNING AND A
NEW LEVEL OF TOUGHNESS

Growing up in Burbank was a wonderful experience, especially when it came to sports. My friends and I played just about everything you can think of. We played whatever professional sport was in season at the time. From football in the street, where we'd all pretend to be Johnny Unitas, to baseball at Pacific Park, where we'd try to catch balls over our backs like Willie Mays—you name it, we did it. During the weekends, we would usually start playing early in the morning, go all day, head home for dinner, and stay out until our parents dragged us inside to sleep—then the next day, we would start all over again.

Although baseball, basketball, and football were all sports I enjoyed, my natural talent lay in running (though I didn't fully realize it until the tenth grade). Everyone has a moment, or a series of moments, that they look back at later in life and realize that's what started them down their career path. For me, those moments were on the blacktops of our elementary school during lunch time. For whatever reason, my friends and I would run laps around the school and time ourselves. Not only did I find this a great challenge and great fun, but because I was the fastest amongst my friends, it was also extremely satisfying. And as elementary school became middle school, I told Dad how much I enjoyed running and he immediately started taking me to track meets around town. When he took me to the Los Angeles Coliseum in the summer of 1964 to watch Team USA take on the Russian national team, little did I know

I would see the man who would go on to have the biggest influence on how I would train for years to come.

Gerry Lindgren was known in running circles around the country as a true prodigy. Training thirty to forty miles a day (not a week, a *day*), Lindgren would run 8:40 for two miles indoors in high school (a race in which he broke the national high school record by forty-three seconds), and as an eighteen-year-old, represented the US as we the faced the Russians at the Los Angeles Coliseum. Competing against the USSR's best distance runners, and in front of a crowd that totaled 50,000 (including Bobby Kennedy), Lindgren went right to the front, powered through the last mile, and ended up winning the race—adding to a dominating Team USA victory. Seeing this scrawny, somewhat nerdy high schooler from Washington take down the best in the world was something I held with me for my life.

As stated, Lindgren liked to run big miles. While learning more about him, I discovered that all the elite guys back then were doing the same. 170, 190, 200 miles-per-week were just the norm for them. And not only did they run a lot, they ran hard. When I began my own running career and learned more about training, my big miles and intense training stemmed from Gerry and others of his generation.

When I met Gerry at the 1970 Olympic Training Camp in Pullman, Washington, he validated everything I'd always thought about training: that it needed to be done *a lot,* and it should almost always be done intensely. Although he was a little different than what I expected (some would call him crazy, I didn't think so—he was just really into training), his concentration, how hard he ran, and how much he ran, were all things I tried to emulate for years to come.

Upon entering high school, my lessons in toughness continued when I met the Burbank High School's cross country coach, Frank Kallem. Kallem was in his early twenties when he began coaching at Burbank, and his calm, cool, and relatable demeanor made him an instant draw for everyone he met. During the mid-1960s and into the 1980s, Burbank High School was one of the great dynasties in American high school cross country and track, with multiple California Interscholastic Federation (CIF) team and individual champions, including the national high school two-mile record holder, Jeff Nelson, who ran 8:36 in 1979 (a record that would stand for another twenty-nine years). So, if you made the varsity team at Burbank, you were a part of a special group. The team's success stemmed from both its great coaching and the team's core values: commitment, aggression, and toughness. Because my parents already enforced these values at home, the cross country team ended up being a great fit for my personality. Making it onto the team and starting my running career, however, happened somewhat by accident.

TOUGHNESS REDEFINED: MY FIRST PRACTICE

Although I really enjoyed running, I had made the decision going into high school that I was going to try out for the football team. The football coach had told me I had a chance of making the B-team, the equivalent of junior varsity, as a place kicker. But before football workouts started that fall, the coach suggested I run with the cross country team during the summer to stay in shape. I had no idea what cross country was, how far they ran, or that the team had the reputation it did. So, one evening after a family dinner that included meat, potatoes, and whole milk, Dad drove me to Griffith Park in downtown L.A. (the place where I would end up running over 25,000 miles during my career, occasionally in the pitch dark) to my first practice.

I had two friends from junior high who were trying out for the team and my only thought going into practice was that I wanted to either stay up with or beat both of them. The coaches sent us out, and at the two-and-a-half-mile marker, I stared to throw up. For the rest of the run, I dry-heaved about every mile. Although I felt like I was going to die during most of the run, it never entered my mind to quit. And after six long, hellacious miles, I finished with one of my buddies—and beat another. As I sat in a pool of my own sweat and vomit after having finished, Coach Kallem made his way over and asked if I was going to try out for the team. I let him know I wasn't there to try out, but to get in shape for football. Once he stopped laughing at my response, he told me I should try out, as he thought I could make the varsity. His statement was dumbfounding; in the history of Burbank High, there were only two boys who had made the varsity team as sophomores (high school back then began in the tenth grade). Those words would alter my life.

I got in the car that night and told my dad that I'd decided I wasn't going to play football and was going to try to make the varsity cross country team instead. He wasn't too excited at first, as he'd really wanted me to play football and baseball. (I still would play summer baseball with my friends, but I got worse and worse at it as I began to take running more seriously.) I truly believed what Coach Kallem had said—that I could make the varsity and that running was something I could excel at. And because of what I had been taught by my parents, once I started something, I was all in and ready to give the best effort I possibly could. Little did I know that this journey would be less about how to become a better runner, and more about the lessons I would carry with me for the next fifty years.

A CULTURE OF TOUGHNESS

Once I joined the team, I started to attend practice regularly and ran on my own when we didn't meet as a team. When Dad couldn't make it home in time to drive me to practice (Mom never learned how to drive), older guys from the team would come and pick me up. I really had no idea what I was doing at the time when it came to training, but just like at home when my parents asked me to do something, when Coach Kallem or older guys on the team told you to run, that's what you did.

The culture of toughness at Burbank High was something that had already been established long before I got there, and would be there for years after. It wasn't about hazing or belittling teammates, but rather about a leader like Kallem who made it clear what needed to be done. His no-nonsense attitude was capped off by a group of guys who not only wanted to succeed, but to work with one another to make the group better.

There was also a level of expectation that came with being a member of the team. Although we only met two days a week during the summer, the better guys trained for six. You were expected to be on time to practice, to train on your own when we didn't meet, and to hold yourself accountable for the work you either did or did not do. The team was successful not just due to talent, but because they knew what it took to be great and did what they needed to do to make it happen. It was an environment in which anyone, if they dedicated themselves enough, could succeed.

At Burbank—whether you ran on a blacktop surface, a rocky road, or a dirt path—you ran barefoot, even during competitions. If you wore shoes on those teams, you were not considered one of *the guys*. The team felt that not wearing shoes set them apart from everyone else. It was part of the culture of toughness. Going barefoot made you stand out against the competition, and the guys were convinced it made you *feel* tougher. This simple act made other teams view us in a different light. Their pre-race focus was usually turned to us, rather than the race itself, because they couldn't get over barefoot cross country runners and the ease with which we competed without sneakers. And at the end of my sophomore year, I learned exactly how important it was that I buy into this philosophy.

The day of our league cross country championship, my first championship race in high school, I decided I was going to wear shoes. That was a big race for me at the time, as myself and teammate Ron Grienel were the two best sophomores on the junior varsity team. Kallem had informed us that whoever was the number one man between the two of us was going to run in the CIF Championship with the varsity. After seeing it was a particularly muddy course we'd be racing on at La Cresenta Park, I decided to warm up in shoes to see if it would give me an advantage. Feeling confident I was going to wear shoes after wearing them for my warmup jog, I did a few more strides with shoes, then decided to do a few barefoot to see what the difference would feel like. When I got back to where my shoes were supposed to be, they were gone. After scrambling to find them, I found out that members of the varsity team had taken them. When I asked for them back, they told me, "Look, we don't wear shoes here. You want to be on this team, this is something you are just gonna deal with. You are either one of us or you are not. We don't want anyone running with us at the CIF meet who is not one of us."

We all have decisions we make, be it a few times a day, once a week, or twice a year, that challenge our level of commitment and toughness. If toughness was deciding to do something I did not want to do, that moment had just been presented to me. I really thought shoes would make a difference for me that day, but after considering the consequences for a few seconds, I knew what was the right thing to do. I was going to become one of *the guys*.

I went on to win the race, run with the varsity at the CIF meet, and I never raced in shoes until my senior year, when the State High School Association created a rule stating that you had to wear shoes during meets. And we did—we just wore gymnastic slippers.

> QUESTION: Describe the culture within your organization or team. Can you name its core values?

Running without shoes back then wasn't the greatest sign of intelligence (a statement I would use to describe The Streak many years later). However, it did accomplish one thing: it helped emphasize what our culture at Burbank was about—commitment, aggression, and toughness beyond everyone else. Now, I'm not suggesting that you train barefoot or put your organization in odd situations to make them tougher. But when you are the leader of a group, you need to create a culture built around a set of core values that you and your team believe in. At Burbank High, our culture was about being tough, believing in ourselves, and persevering no matter the odds. When things didn't work out, we always asked ourselves: Could I have been tougher? Could I have believed in myself more? When things got hard, did I persevere or did I give in?

"We had some great individuals on teams at Burbank over the thirty-plus years I was lucky enough to be there. It began with Rick Romero in 1962, who won the CIF Championship in the Mile, barefoot, running 4:14. We tried to instill a toughness in our kids that was centered around being aggressive, training hard, and laying it all out on race days. Mark [Covert] really personified those values when he was with our team. He was extremely tenacious in how he trained and competed, putting his body through things both in competition and training that no one else was willing to experience. At Burbank, we created a program that was so tough, people didn't want to race against us. And I think that is the persona Mark carried with him throughout his entire career."

Frank Kallem
Head track & cross country coach,
Burbank High School, 1962–2000
School Records during the Kallem era:
Half-Mile: 1:50
Mile: 4:07
Two-Mile: 8:36 (National Two-Mile Record)

To create a culture that is sustainable and continually holds people accountable, everyone in your organization needs to know your group's core values. You cannot have an effective culture unless everyone is on the same page. And if you are a member of a team, you need to have a full understanding of the principals that make your team what it is. You need to be about something. Doing something just for the sake of doing it doesn't create an atmosphere that leads to winning.

There is a saying that "one bad apple spoils a bunch." This could not be more accurate when it comes to having a few people out of sync with the values of your organization. When I warmed up in shoes, I wasn't in tune with one of the values of the program, which in turn resulted in guys on the team questioning my commitment. Once I made the decision to get myself in line, not only did I become more accepted amongst the guys on the team, but it made my entire experience easier and more enjoyable; we were now all on the same page when it came to what was expected of us and how things needed to be done.

BELIEVING IN YOURSELF (AND GETTING OTHERS TO DO THE SAME)

Kallem taught us that in order to be tough when it really mattered, you needed to believe in yourself. Coach was incredibly inspirational, not just for me, but for a generation of athletes that would come through the Burbank High running program. With Kallem as a coach, you actually wanted to come to practice, *and* to keep training on days the team didn't meet, because he could relate things to the team in an exciting and unique way that made you want to run your best, not just for yourself, but for the people around you.

QUESTION: Do the people with whom you surround yourself help you believe in yourself and make you want to become the best you can be? If not, what can you do to change that?

So much of instilling faith in others starts with communicating effectively. You can't be a successful leader if you don't know how to communicate in a way people can relate to. There was never any question about what needed to be accomplished during a practice session or a meet day at Burbank High, because Kallem always explained things in a way that was clear and to the point. And if he needed to kick you in the butt for not doing what he asked, he would be there immediately afterward to put his arm around you, encourage you, and make sure you understood where he was coming from.

Kallem was also an outstanding motivator, not just in the way he spoke to us, but in what he said and when. He continually emphasized how great we could be because of the work that we had put in. 20 x 400 m was a staple workout for us; so was 20 x 200 m, along with being dropped off twelve miles from school and having to run back. Although Burbank did not become a program that ran big miles until after I left, the workouts were challenging, and we still did more work than nearly anyone in the area. Once we'd done all the work, Kallem had us believing we could do anything.

Much of gaining belief in oneself goes back to the preparation I mentioned earlier. If you are prepared, you have a platform to be as tough as you want to be. You can decide to be tougher than the person standing next to you because you have put in more time, more work, and in the case of the Burbank High team, more *challenging* work than them. When you add belief to preparation, commitment, and positive self-talk—that's a hard combination to beat. Because I listened to and believed in my coach and what he taught me, it was easier to believe in myself and what I could do.

QUESTION: What do you do to make others believe in you?

USING VISUALIZATION TO BECOME TOUGHER

Kallem was also a big proponent of visualization and I found it to be an extremely helpful tool in not only my preparation but also my confidence. Visualization for me became another piece to toughness and something I would use for the rest of my racing career. Before many competitions, after a workout, we would all lie down, close our eyes, and walk through the race before it happened. When we first started to do this, the team laughed hard at Kallem. But once we started to really utilize it and see its benefits, the laughter subsided, and the preparation began. We would visualize every scenario, every turn in the course, and go over the plan for the upcoming meet. From how the course would feel on our bare feet to which way the wind was more likely to blow—Kallem worked diligently to paint for us the most detailed picture of the competition imaginable.

I believe visualization made us tougher, even more prepared, and more confident going into meets—especially big ones. On race day when we arrived at the course, we had the confidence of knowing that mentally we had already competed (and won) in that day's meet. Our anxiety about what may happen that day was gone and the only thing that sat in our minds was how we were going to execute. I continued to use a visualization routine throughout my career before races, during warm-ups, and even during competition when I felt my anxiety getting a bit high. I felt it added another layer of toughness to my competitive armor.

Currently, especially within the running community, visualization training and mental conditioning are not utilized as frequently as they should be. While this component of training has taken on a vital role in football, baseball, and basketball, the mental side of training is still very much lacking in track and cross country. Many running coaches believe that just chatting about the race prior to the gun going off is all you need to be mentally prepared. Although this is important, I don't believe it's enough. There is nothing wrong with taking time to prepare your emotions, train your mind, and teach yourself how to deal with current and future stress. Visit www.thestreakbook.com for a free visualization session.

Whether you are in the business world while preparing for a big presentation, a football player getting ready for a playoff game, or a sprinter heading into a preliminary round race, having trained your mind to be at its best can be the difference between moving on to the next round or watching it from the stands.

Across all disciplines, there are three segments a person can train: a specific skill set, your body, and your mind. Kallem had us training physically at a high intensity, while simultaneously communicating with us how we needed to be thinking—especially when we started to become exhausted. Rather than telling us to suck it up when we felt like death or giving us a motivational line that would inspire us for just a matter of seconds, he spoke about calming our breathing, quieting our mind, and staying in the moment—all tools that were taught to us during our visualization sessions.

QUESTION: Describe what you do to train your mind. How much time do you allocate to it each day?

Visualization also made me more aware of my body, my emotions, and the situations I was stepping into. It made me more alert of potential scenarios, allowed me to effectively examine my emotions, and helped me to enhance my focus. I would go over what we visualized in our pre-meet sessions while I warmed up, especially in certain parts of the course where things could be tough. Then I'd focus on crossing the finish line, where I would imagine out-kicking some guys to the line, or even winning the race. I found this extremely helpful in keeping my nerves down, teaching me to stay focused in the moment, and most importantly, building my confidence. Especially in situations where I felt my body was about to break, having already experienced a scenario in my head, I felt like I could deal with it effectively and not have it end my race. And when others panicked, my preparation helped me to keep calm and allowed me to succeed.

TAKING RISKS

The final piece to toughness is what I believe is its most crucial element—your ability and willingness to take risks, or your ability to "go for it." **I define risk as doing something in which your return on investment can be high, but your chance for failure is higher.** Much like toughness—"doing something you don't want to do"—risk can look different depending on the situation you are in. If you have ever taken a risk, you achieved something in the face of fear. If the result was not what you were hoping for, you may have felt emotional or physical pain immediately afterward. This is the main reason people tend not to go for it; they are afraid of getting hurt.

If you are going to be successful, you can't be afraid to hurt. That hurt can come from getting no sleep while studying for an exam, cramping up after a hard workout, or getting rejected by someone you have feelings for. Whatever the case may be, going for it tends to separate the average people who never reach their potential from the great ones who always take chances to see how great they are.

When I was competing, especially when I was first beginning my running career, I never wanted to walk away from a race knowing I let fear take control and negatively affect my body, my emotions, or my effort. I fully understood that I *could* fail; but rather than run away from those feelings, I took them as signals that gave me the green light to really get after it.

For yourself, whether it's a difficult conversation with a loved one, deciding to make a big move during your next race, or simply trying something new for the first time, if you are not willing to be open to potential failure, there is a good chance you will never learn how good you can be.

Much of your ability to take risks comes from knowing **you can only control those things that are controllable.** There are certain things you can control (which need your attention) and then there are things you have no control over at all (these things are not worth your time). You've got to recognize the difference between the two and how to react differently to them. Kallem always made it clear that we could never control what the competition would do on race day. The same went for the conditions of the course, or how we felt on that particular day; however, we could *always* control our effort and our focus.

There are lots of things others control, but your effort is the one thing you are always in total control of. It doesn't matter what others do or say, it's you and you alone who can either coast along or compete with the kind of resolution that makes you great. There are people in the world who will always have incredible amounts of skill and natural talent—but unless they combine that talent with consistent effort, those who try harder will take them down every time. You can control your effort and emotions

24/7. Learning to master that control may be tough at times, but it will pay off greatly in the long term.

I quickly learned that thinking about how other people performed, how they felt, or even how talented they were compared to me was waste of my time. Sitting around worrying about uncontrollables took focus away from what I needed to do that day to be my best. Later in my career—whether it was racing against Steve Prefontaine at the National Cross Country Championships or Frank Shorter at the Olympic Trials—I focused on doing the best with what I had. When I kept the attention on myself, I wasn't worried about how the competition felt that day, what they had done previously, or what they may be able to do during that race.

During the 1960s, high school cross country races were only two-miles (compared to now where races last between three miles and 5,000 meters). You needed to have some courage to get yourself in the front of the race early or your chances of winning dwindled rapidly. Getting out fast was perfect for our team's personality, as being fearless played a significant role in our identity as "tough guys" at Burbank. Coach Kallem always made it clear that nothing was going on in the back of the race (or the back of anything for the matter); to succeed you wanted to be in front with the lead pack, in the front row of the classroom, or at the front of anything you did. He was convinced that you would never be great if you did not put yourself right into the mix and see how you could do.

My dad preached the same thing to my brother and me growing up. Even if I did not win the race that day, the most important thing I could do was to put in my best effort. When I completed a race, a test, or even a game with my friends, I needed to know I did my best. And that is what taking risks is really all about.

QUESTION: Would you consider yourself a risk taker? If so, what makes you think so? If you aren't, what are the things that hinder your ability to "go for it"?

FINAL THOUGHTS ON TOUGHNESS

Toughness, at the end of the day, is about choice. You and only you can decide how committed you are going to be, if you are going to prepare correctly, and how you are going to communicate with yourself. You are the one who has to choose if you are going to train your mind, if you'll believe in yourself, and if you are going to go for it.

Right now, in this very moment, and in each moment that follows, you can make the choice to be as tough as you want to be—to go on a run you haven't attempted before, to push yourself harder than you did last time, to study more, to commit more, to love more. The choice is yours. The question isn't *what* you are going to do to become tougher, the question is whether you are going to *do* the things that can get you there. As I went through high school, I was continually presented with scenarios that tested my toughness. And just like Dad with his knives, I found the tools to hone and sharpen it.

Question: What choice can you make **right now** that will allow you to become tougher?

Mom and Dad in 1960

PART II
I WILL MAKE YOU A MAN

TIME FRAME:
October 31, 1968–November 28, 1970
TOTAL DAYS RUN CONSECUTIVELY: 1,095
TOTAL CAREER MILES RUN: 17,743
BIGGEST MILEAGE WEEK: 215
TOTAL CAREER DISTANCE COVERED:
The equivalent of 7,097.2 laps at Daytona Speedway
HISTORY:
- The Doors release their first album
- The Green Bay Packers win Super Bowl I
- Martin Luther King, Jr., is assassinated
- Robert F. Kennedy is assassinated
- Tommie Smith & John Carlos protest at the 1968 Olympics
- Neil Armstrong walks on the moon
- The Beatles release *Abbey Road,* their final album
- 100,000 people protest the Vietnam War in Washington DC

I ran every day.

IT BEGINS

The Streak didn't begin with me waking up one July morning fully committed to running each day for the next forty-five years. In a way, just like how I joined the team at Burbank, it happened by accident.

I can't discuss The Streak without mentioning my journal, because it's how I found out The Streak was alive. Starting when I was a sophomore in high school, all the way until The Streak's final day, I kept a written record of every run and workout I did. My journal would be a major key to my success for the next forty-five years. Inside its pages, I would record what I did that day, how many miles I ran, and how I felt. From that I could see what worked in my training and (perhaps most importantly) what didn't.

I made certain I didn't lie to myself when I journaled, as I found being honest with myself when it came to training (and everything else) was vital to achieving my goals. That self-honesty became the accountability system I needed to help keep me on task. When I taught fitness classes in the 1970s, I always told students who were looking to lose weight to keep an eating and workout journal. It allowed them to have their own personal coach who didn't talk back or tell them they were failing. That journal showed them what they had done when they began to see progress or when things started to fall off.

I think everyone should keep a journal, whether they are an athlete, out to achieve a personal goal, or wanting to succeed in their profession. And as important as my coaches and teammates were in keeping me accountable for the work I needed to do, it was the simple action of putting pen to paper each day that made all the difference.

> QUESTION: Do you keep a journal?
> Either for your workouts or personal thoughts?

In October of 1968, I checked my journal and realized I had gone 100 days without taking a day off from training. The last day I'd missed was July 23, 1968. When I noticed this, I thought to myself, "I wonder if I can get to a year without missing a day." So, from that point on, hurt, sick, or whatever the situation was, I did what I needed to get my run in. I figured if it went on for a year, that would be a great accomplishment. I never let the prospect of running every day for a year scare me. Lots of people I knew had made promises to themselves, but few kept them, and I never wanted to be one of those people. Still, if I didn't make it because of an injury or illness, at least I could go to sleep at night knowing I'd tried.

When I finally reached a year of running every day, it was the summer of 1969. Getting out each morning and working out didn't feel like a burden. In fact, waking up each morning to go for a run was exciting. There was a visceral sensation that came over me each time I laced up my shoes that could only be described as thrilling. Improving myself each day, while others sat at home and dreaded working out, was as great for my confidence as it was for my legs. Not only was I tougher and more prepared than anyone else, I never had an excuse for not performing well.

Another reason I didn't want to skip any days during the early part of The Streak was because I still had a burning desire to be one of "the guys." I didn't just want to be the best on whatever team I happened to be on at the time—I wanted to be the best on *any* team. I would frequently look at the results from meets in *Track & Field News* and thought that the more I trained and the less time I missed, the greater my chances to compete against, and maybe even beat, some of the best runners in the country. Even if I was not the best on any given day (and when I started, I certainly wasn't), putting in the work to get there was what drove me to keep trying.

Although many were amazed by The Streak in those early days, most thought it was foolish. But once people found out I had stopped missing days, they began to view me as someone who was durable, able to train hard over and over without breaking. As someone who always desired to be viewed as a tough guy, these new opinions helped shape my confidence as I entered the next phase of my running journey at L.A. Valley Junior College.

L.A. VALLEY, LASZLO TABORI, AND THREE-HOUR WORKOUTS

Coming out of Burbank High, I was offered a scholarship to run at San Fernando Valley State College (which later would become California State University, Northridge). The scholarship itself was a parking pass that equated to four dollars per semester. Although I was flattered to be offered anything at all, I thought I could do a bit better than a parking pass as a scholarship. So, with that, I decided to enroll at Los Angeles Valley College, running for Head Coach George Ker and his assistant, Laszlo Tabori. Valley had a pretty good team at that time that included:

- Mike Wagenbach (4:25 miler out of Notre Dame High School, who ended up running 4:04 in the mile at Long Beach State)
- Jim Estes (from Monroe High School, who would run 4:07 in the mile and 1:51 in the 800m at Valley)
- Manuel "Manny" Green (from Hollywood High, who would run 1:53 in the 800m at Valley and was a key member of our 4 x 400m relay teams)
- And two guys who didn't run blazing times, but were tough competitors, Bobby King and Howard Miller.

Although our team was loaded, I felt that with my training that summer (which grew from around 200 miles-per-month during high school to above 600 each month the summer before my first collegiate season), I might have had a chance to run with the better guys on the team.

Our first practice took place in Santa Monica during the summer of 1969. Going into the workout, I had been running fifteen miles in the morning and fifteen miles at night. Even though some of the runs were not as fast as I would have liked, I was in the best shape of my life up to that point. And mentally, I was ready to be up with the top guys on the team for each workout and every race.

Coach Ker met with us at L.A. Valley and drove us down to San Vicente Boulevard. Although it was a busy street, it had a long strip of grass running between the east and west lanes, and due to the consistently nice weather and forgiving surface, that was a popular place to run. The entire team was present and being the new guy who didn't want to get his ass kicked, I had taken my runs a bit easier for a few days going into the workout.

We started the run going downhill at the top of San Vicente Boulevard, across Ocean Avenue, down to the Santa Monica Pier, and back up the long, gradual uphill to where we started—around twelve miles total. After staying with the group up to the turnaround point, I decided I was going to try to turn it on and see what would happen. I pushed really hard that second half of the run and ended up beating everyone by several minutes. When we got back to the car, my confidence couldn't have been higher, as the guys on the team were shocked that I'd kicked *their* asses. Knowing the talent level of the guys in that group (especially Wagenbach and Estes) and seeing how badly I'd beat them really gave me the shot of adrenaline I needed going into my next challenge as an athlete. To my surprise the real challenge wasn't racing at the collegiate level—it was training with Laszlo Tabori.

Laszlo was the third person in recorded history to run under 4:00 in the mile. He was also the former world record holder in the 4x1,500m, and 1,500m, and while representing Hungary in the 1956 Olympics, he'd finished fourth in the 1,500m and sixth in the 5,000m. After the Olympics, he and several other Hungarian athletes had defected to the United States, settled in L.A., and continued their training. At that point Tabori, even as he continued to train, mostly focused on coaching at Valley as an assistant under Coach Ker and trained amateur athletes with the San Fernando Valley Track Club. After having witnessed a few workouts given by Coach Tabori while I was in high school, I knew that if I wasn't in shape, I was going to be in deep shit—his style of training was different than anything anyone in the US was doing at the time.

As most runners in the States would train by going on aerobic runs and mixing in interval training a few days a week, *everything* Tabori did was intervals on the track—with most workouts lasting between two and three hours. I'm not making this up so you'll continue reading this book; this is how we trained six days a week. And for myself, as someone who believed in running big miles, I would also add a five- to ten-mile run either early in the morning or late at night.

On the last day of The Streak, I made a joke that Laszlo (who was standing next to me at the time) did better than anyone or anything else, to end it. Each one of those workouts, in their own unique way, were *hard*. Most workouts started at 5:00 p.m. and didn't end until after 7:30 p.m.

Jackie Hansen, my good friend who would become the third female winner of the Boston Marathon and a world record holder, was also coached by Lazslo. After the nearly forty-minute warm-up of her first workout, she grabbed her clothes and began to walk to her car, thinking the workout was over. She was wrong of course—the workout itself went on for another two hours. But don't think that just because the training was hard we didn't come ready to go on race day. No one had us more prepared on meet days than Lazslo.

"I basically learned all of my life lessons from Laszlo Tabori. He taught me about commitment, dedication, perseverance—all the skills you need to deal with the ups and downs of life, I learned from him during those hours we spent on the track. But perhaps the most important thing he taught me is that great leaders can be tough, strict, and fair. Most think it's impossible to have all three of these traits—Laszlo proved you could. He was fair to everyone. If you showed up on time and did the work, he would put everything he could into your wanting to be successful. And as a woman running in the 1970s when the Olympics didn't allow women to run over 800 meters, when I expressed interest in wanting to run the Marathon, he didn't tell me no—he told me he thought I could go far. Turned out, he was right."

Jackie Hansen
Third Woman to Win the Boston Marathon
Two-time World Record Holder, Women's Marathon
Two-time Master's World Track Champion
Former President, International Runners Committee, the group responsible for successfully lobbying the IOC to add Women's events for 5,000m, 10,000m, and the Marathon to the Olympic Games

A week after my first run with the team on San Vicente Boulevard, we did our first workout as a group with Tabori. After leading the workout, he came over to me and asked if I was going to start training with the team each day. After affirming that I would be there every day, he grabbed me by the arm as hard as he could, pulled me in about one inch from his face, looked at me dead in the eye, and, as if he were giving me military orders, said, **"If you train with me, I will make you a man."**

First Workout with Tabori during the Summer of 1968:
- 2-mile warm-up jog
- 15 x 110m strides
- 5 x 250m
- 5 x 400m
- 1 x 1000m [last 200 HARD]
- 6 x 150m
- 1 x 1000m [last 200 HARD]
- 2 x 200m [VERY HARD]
- 1 x 250m build
- 12 x 110m
- 2-mile cool-down
  All of the workout, including the warm-up and cool-down, was done on the track

At the time, I had no idea what Lazslo was talking about. But as days of practice turned into weeks of training, I realized what he meant: that if I worked with him, **I would become the best version of myself.** When you worked with Tabori, being your best was mandatory, or you simply would not survive a day of training. There was no faking it and no taking repetitions off. For you to train at that level, you needed to be at your best—all the time. Trying to pretend you were someone else as a survival technique was not an effective solution. You needed to be fully committed to being the very best version of yourself—on every single repetition of every single day of practice. That was the only way you'd get better. Training in this manner not only made us more confident as athletes, it made us better in all aspects of our lives.

Lazslo's teachings made me realize that being the best version of oneself requires three critical elements: **eliminating excuses, focusing on one task at a time, and increasing your level of commitment.** Understanding these elements both individually and collectively was vital in my growth not just as a runner, but as a person.

ELIMINATING EXCUSES

Everyone has excuses. When I trained, even though I didn't skip any days, I had plenty of excuses for why I didn't need to train hard on certain days. Rather than run fifteen miles, I might just run eleven if my legs felt dead. If I'd had a rough night's sleep, I could easily pull that excuse out of the hat if I had a crappy morning training session. However, I never let my excuses become chronic and I didn't let them get in my way of my long-term goals.

Each day at Valley, my goals were the same: win that day's practice, become the Junior College State Champion in cross country, and get a scholarship to a four-year school.

Even when training got challenging or my times were not what I had hoped, I never pointed fingers at others. I knew I had control of every situation I'd placed myself in and creating excuses was simply a way of deflecting my shortcomings onto someone else. No positive results ever came out of blaming people who weren't at fault.

I define excuses as **obstacles that get in the way of what needs to be done.** Like I mentioned before, excuses are things we all use sometimes. It's not a problem to have an excuse every once in a while; that's not the issue. It's when those excuses become repetitive that things can start to go south almost immediately. Once you miss one day, it becomes okay to miss a second day, and then a third; you can just fall back on the excuse used to miss day one. This is when excuses become a part of your life and your short- and long-term goals can escape you.

Me as a senior at
Burbank High School

If you're looking to succeed in school, taking a day off from class simply because you feel like it will hinder your success in that class. Missing a day of work when you have a lot on your plate because you would rather catch up on sleep can hinder your ability to get your work done the following day; the work doesn't magically disappear while you're asleep.

TRAINING, THE TABORI WAY

Much like my parents, Tabori believed excuses were bullshit. If you had a rough day at school, work, or in life, that was no reason to get out of something. You weren't allowed days off just because things were shitty. An excuse was a rock that could be moved, not a mountain that couldn't be.

> QUESTION: How often do you use excuses? In what scenario (work, training, life) do you use them the most? When you use them, are the reasons legitimate, or is it because you want to take the easiest path to get out of something?

Tabori showed me that when I needed to be at my absolute best, there was never a reason or an excuse not to believe in myself, put in my best effort, and see how successful I could be that day. Even when I was sick or injured, I never used that as an excuse. A fitting example took place at our second cross country meet of 1969 at Whittier College. Along with several other great teams, San

Diego State (which no longer has men's cross country or track teams) joined us at the meet—and they were loaded. Several men on their team had ran under 8:48 for the two-mile, and their top runner was Tim Danielson, who was the third high schooler in US history to run under 4:00 in the mile.

Tabori's strategy for us was the same going into that race as it was for everyone he coached us through. Later, I'd use the same school of thought during my entire running and coaching career. His philosophy was simple: get to the front of the race and when the time is right, just kick their ass. If you weren't doing that, you simply weren't pushing hard enough.

The race itself was challenging. The course was five miles and included fences you needed to jump over, gates you had to run through, and some rough terrain—a little different from the pristine courses college athletes run today. During the last mile, the top guys got away from me and I ended up finishing third amongst individuals, with our team finishing third overall.

Although we didn't win, our team was the talk of the meet due to our willingness to mix it up with the better guys and hang in there for as long as we did. For us, this was no surprise. After surviving weeks of multi-hour workouts with Tabori, no one felt like they couldn't go toe-to-toe with any team from any division across the country. More importantly, no one had an excuse on the starting line or after the meet that permitted them to take the easy way out. We all had put in the work, were confident in ourselves, and we expected to be great.

As we all improved and became more confident under Tabori's training, our ability to eliminate excuses and embrace new challenges grew. This was especially useful when the meets started to really matter—like one against our arch-rival, Pasadena City College, on their home course during my first year at Valley. Just like most community college teams in California back then, Pasadena's team was chock full of studs. And what made the meet even more intriguing was that we had beaten them the week before at the Long Beach State Invitational.

At the one-mile marker of the four-mile race, with lots of pushing and shoving taking place, I got tangled up and fell ass-over-head into the dirt. I popped right up, bleeding from a cut on my face that turned my white singlet into a dirt-covered, blood-drenched rag. I had only lost a few steps to the lead pack. Halfway through the race, however, I lost focus and was about fifty yards back from the leader. Tabori was pissed off when he saw where I was and yelled for me to stop feeling sorry for myself. I did what I was told, ignored the blood, blocked out the pain, and pushed myself back up with the leader.

I won the race by ten seconds.

That win put the fear of God in people and secured my reputation. My perseverance that day proved that no matter the obstacle—falling, bleeding, down by fifty yards—you couldn't count me out of any race. Our team, however, lost to Pasadena that day and would lose to them again at the Mount San Antonio College (Mount SAC) Invitational the following week. It took a while, but we would eventually beat them during the championship part of the season.

That incident and the many great battles we had over the next two years were some of the best experiences I had as a junior college athlete.

> QUESTION: What are some examples of when you eliminated excuses to succeed? How did the result make you feel?

ONE TASK AT A TIME

When you arrived at the track to train with Tabori, you really didn't know what to expect other than a ton of running at a very high intensity. If today's coaches saw our workouts from back then, they would first, think we were crazy, and second, see about two to three days of work squeezed into one session. **Although they were challenging, Tabori's workout sessions taught us a skill that separated our team from others across the state—the ability to focus on one task at a time.** You wouldn't be able to last long in those workouts if you were focused on how hard or long they were. Instead, you had to focus on the interval that was right in front of you and not concern yourself with how dead you were or how much you had left in the session. And that type of concentration exercise made race day a piece of cake when it came to focus.

The ability to focus on one thing at a time was a tool we learned to utilize in nearly every aspect of our lives, and is something I still preach today. For example, if you have to balance family, school, and work, it's much more productive to focus on the immediate task, rather than trying to get everything over with at once. This is critical if you want to be at your best and show others they matter, as well. Your friends, family, teammates, and boss all expect you to be fully engaged. No one likes to be half attended to or engage in conversations where one person's head is in another place. They need you to be right there, focused on them and their concerns.

A key element to living life one task at a time is being able to focus on the *process* rather than the *outcome*. The results matter, but it's the work that's done each day that requires the largest amount of your attention. Elite runners obsess about the day-to-day training, about improving, about doing everything they can to be *prepared* to be at their best come race day. This is what it looks like to live life one task at a time; not dwelling on the memories of past losses, not imagining how great things may be when the current task is over, but rather focusing on the most important part of your journey—the step that is right in front of you.

When you begin living life one task at a time, you will become more mindful of your body and emotions. If all you think about is what has already happened or what may happen, how can you do your best and adjust in the moment? (I'll answer that one for you—you can't, because you don't know what the hell is going on.) When your mind strays away from the moment, you can get lost in a sea of past failures, potential outcomes, and thoughts that do nothing to help you succeed. Even if you are tired and ready to quit, you can still achieve remarkable things by developing and then utilizing skills that keep you grounded in the moment to get the job done.

One evening, during one of Tabori's three-hour workout sessions, someone made the comment that the group was feeling tired. He stopped us right then and screamed, "You're *tired?*" After everyone communicated (in one way or another) that were we all drained, he proclaimed, "Ha! I was tired for ten years! 400 in sixty seconds—go!" It didn't matter how tired we were. It didn't matter how we felt from the previous intervals. What mattered to Tabori was what happened in that moment. He knew that for us to achieve our goals, we had to learn that even though we were tired, nothing good could be accomplished if we weren't thinking about the task at hand.

> QUESTION: Do you and your organization or team focus on the process or the outcome? Do you think about the goal at the end of the road or the object that is right in front of you?

The next time you dream about winning that big game, killing that presentation, or acing an exam, stop and think about where your legs are. Wherever you are standing is where your focus should be. The best and most effective thing you can focus on is *this* practice, *this* presentation, or *this* study session. Putting all your effort into the task immediately in front of you will help you eliminate excuses and make that next moment all the better and more rewarding. The quickest way to head down the path of success is to focus on the current step, no matter what the rest of the road looks like.

INCREASING YOUR LEVEL OF COMMITMENT

Commitment and hard work are emphasized on every team. It doesn't matter if it's a small business, large corporation, college football team, or high school cross country team—coaches and team members always discuss the importance of working hard and staying committed. But *successful* teams (and individuals) understand how to put those words into action. Commitment is not just about doing what you are told or working hard; rather it is an understanding that even when you *think* you are putting in everything you can give, you always need to increase your output in order to succeed and not become idle.

I discussed briefly what I learned about commitment as a high school athlete, but when I became a member of the team at Valley and then later at California State University, Fullerton, I discovered that as the challenges became more difficult, my level of commitment needed to increase. Doing what I did in high school just wasn't going to cut it. Training like a seventeen-year-old would not work if I expected to beat guys who were older, more experienced, and more talented. Now, having worked in both athletics and business, I've learned that raising your level of commitment is vital in anything you do when you make the jump to the next level.

Whether you're making the move from the junior varsity to the varsity team, or from junior to senior sales associate, you will be asked to do more work and spend more time than you did in your previous position. If you are naïve enough to think that just because you were successful at one level, you will automatically be just as fortunate at the next, you will more than likely be proven wrong—and quickly. In order to ensure your continued success, you will need to develop new skills, cultivate new relationships, and spend more time training or studying than before. Moderately talented athletes, employees, and students can become exceptional if they elevate their levels of dedication and diligence. (We have all seen this happen before, so don't ever let anyone tell you that it can't.) On our team at Valley, our team's work ethic overcame a lack of raw talent (especially for me, who was in no way considered a "stud" in high school, having only run 9:27 for the two-mile). When our team's diligence was mixed with an unbreakable commitment and desire to be the best, we were hard to beat come race day.

California Junior College State
Cross Country Champion, 1968

> QUESTION: How committed are you and/or your team to being consistent and tough on a day-to-day basis? What could you or they do to be more committed?

One of the reasons I made the decision to bump my miles up to from 200 to 600 a month (besides reading that all the professional runners did the same) was to show my teammates how committed I was to becoming the best I could be. I never wanted anyone to think I was half-in on my training or the team. Later when I was a salesman working fifteen-hour days while on the road 150 days out of the year, I always made that last call at the end of a long day, especially when I didn't want to. I wanted my clients to know I was committed to them—just like I did for my teammates when I was training.

> QUESTION: Consider the major decisions you must make each day. How often do you commit to those decisions? And how often do you break your commitments to yourself and others because that may be easier?

While I was in college, I was a big history buff and, although I received a degree in Physical Education, finished three credits short of a minor in history. The Greek Philosophers always interested me, especially the Stoics, whom Kallem would quote often when I was at Burbank High. One of the many ideas taught by the Stoics (Marcus Aurelius, Seneca, and Cato are some of the best-known) was that we each have control of what is right in front of us; no other person is in control of what we do—we control our reactions and thoughts. This school of thought has been followed and preached by leaders in politics and sports, from George Washington to Phil Jackson.

Victor Frankl, author of the horrific but inspirational memoir of his experience during the Holocaust, *A Man's Search for Meaning,* was also a follower of the Stoics. The statement I found the most enlightening from his book was one that summarized the importance of being in the moment. He believed that within each moment, we have a chance to learn who we truly are. He stated that, **"Between stimulus and response there is space. In that space is our power to choose our response. In our response lies our growth and our freedom."**

Throughout The Streak, and especially during my college days when my legs were dead from high intensity and volume of training, there were lots of times where I could have stayed in bed rather than go out for my run. Each morning during those days, and for the forty-five years that I ran each day, I was presented with two options:

Option 1: Get up and go for my run. (I knew this was the path that led to success, even when I felt like I couldn't do it.)

Option 2: Stay in bed and sleep. (This would serve my immediate need of wanting more rest, but would also allow other people to gain on me when it came to training.)

Although there were days where it was tough to get out of bed, I always made the choice in the morning to lace up my shoes and head out the door (until the day I literally couldn't). That is where learning to eliminate the excuses, staying committed, and focusing one task at a time became valuable weapons against pain and negativity. I didn't want to be one of those people who sat in bed and dreamed about winning a State Cross Country Championship; I wanted to be the person who went out and did it. I also really enjoyed getting out the door each day. Lacing up my shoes and doing something I loved each day was special for me. Just like when I began The Streak, getting up and out for a run was not a burden—it was fun. Even when I was sick or hurt, it was fun to see how far or how hard I could go. That internal challenge that I had with myself each day gave me a great reason to never miss.

Skipping steps along the path to success so you can take the easy way out is just that—easy. But being able to fully commit comes from making the decision that you are going to do something no matter what the circumstances. Once you have committed to something, you need to be in all the way. There is no half-in or half-out. In that moment, when push comes to shove, you have to do whatever you need to do to get the job done. You get things done not by false hopes or shortcuts; you achieve remarkable things because you do the work that needs to get done.

When I started coaching, I always told my team the following on the first day of cross country practice, so that everyone understood the level of commitment I felt was required of them to become a successful member of our team:

"If there is a snow storm, there is still practice. If there is a rain storm, there is still practice. If there is an earthquake,

and the earth is split in half, you better be on my side because there is still practice. There is never an excuse for missing, because there is always practice."

You may think this statement is a little over-the-top, but I took it very seriously; I wanted to make the standards of commitment clear to my team. Unless you were very, very sick, or very, very hurt, there was never a reason you could not be at practice. This was the level of commitment I learned by witnessing my father always go into work and while I was training with Tabori. Once you started something, you did it at 100 percent.

When you are hired to do a job, or chosen to be a member of a team, you are expected to do the job to the maximum of your ability, all the time. It is just like a relationship— once you commit, there is no one else. No matter what the situation, commitment is a block to success that can't be ignored and always should be evaluated.

THE NEXT MOVE

While at Valley, my teammates and I were lucky enough to achieve remarkable things. We were the California Junior College Cross Country State Champions twice and broke the national junior college record in the 4x1 mile relay (a race that I was just happy to be a part of, since I wasn't even close to being the fastest miler on our team). Personally, I won the State Cross Country Championship along with the State Two-Mile Championship on the track, and broke the national junior college record for six miles, becoming the first J.C. runner to run six miles under 29:00.

Because of my success, I was lucky enough to be recruited by colleges and universities from all over the country. Obtaining a four-year degree was important to my parents and me, but being an average student, I wanted to be at a place where I felt I could get the help I needed academically and still compete at a high level athletically. I made the decision in the spring of my sophomore year to attend California State University, Fullerton, which was located about an hour from Burbank in Orange County, California. Even after recruiting trips to the University of Nebraska; the University of Southern California; the University of California, Los Angeles; Stanford College; and Washington State University, I felt that Fullerton would provide great academic support (during a time before schools had tutors and mandatory study halls) and I knew it had a good team. Also, back in those days, if you placed high in the Division II National Championships, you would be able to compete at the Division I National Championships the following week, so I thought it was a great chance to still compete against the best, get an education, and stay close to home.

Although Fullerton was a Division II school at the time, we had one of the best recruiting classes in the country. It included:

- Dave White (from El Medina High School, who ran 8:56 for the two-mile in high school, along with 14:00 for the three-mile);
- Tim Tubb (from Moorpark Junior College, who was as good as any junior college runner in the country);
- John Casso & Jim McGuire (both sub-4:10 milers);

- Doug Schmink (from Golden West Junior College, who, during his senior year at Fullerton, became the youngest US Marathon Champion in history);
- and Curt Thompson (another sub-4:10 miler, who was an outstanding team guy and, even though he would end up being our seventh man in cross country, would run some big races for us when it counted).

When I got to Fullerton, most of the guys on the team were running between 140 and 170 miles a week. And what made that group particularly special to train with was that no one was afraid to do this volume of work, and at a high intensity (much like we did with Tabori at Valley). We had a saying back then that "miles were king," and for us, they most definitely were. The team at Fullerton was also extremely competitive with one another. You didn't just want to have a great session, you wanted to kick your teammates' asses in every repetition at every practice. It created an environment in which practices mirrored race day. If you were the champion of that day's workout, you felt really good about yourself, knowing the caliber of the guys that were on our team.

Fullerton also happened to be a fantastic place to train. During my first year, the 57 freeway had not been built yet, and nearly all our runs took place on horse trails or through orange groves that surrounded campus. The temperatures almost always remained comfortable for our training, in the high fifties in the morning, and in the low seventies in the evenings. And as the community around us continued to grow, we really didn't notice because we were so focused on training. One day as we ran through the orange farms located just east of the campus, we were all nearly run over by a pickup truck that was making its way down the new 57 freeway—which we didn't realize existed.

Our team was mostly junior college transfers, so we weren't like typical four-year college athletes who hoped that by the time we were in our twenties we would be good enough to compete. We all wanted immediate success, which helped strengthen the bonds and the concern we each had for one another. Much like at Burbank, everyone was on the same page about high-intensity training and a desire to do something special, not just as individuals but for one another. As we went into our first cross country season during the fall of 1970, our goals were clear: win a Cross Country National Championship and, while doing so, beat the hell out of anyone who stood in our way.

THE MIGHTY TITANS

Our training philosophy at CSU Fullerton was simple: train a lot and don't be scared to train hard—which was something I'd grown accustomed to; it was the only way I knew how to train. Now, because no one told us to slow down or run less, I'm sure some of our best days were left at practice. Still, this type of training made us Titans so confident that even if we were tired on race day, we had the mental fortitude to push through without much of a problem.

This rare type of freedom in our training was due to our head cross country coach, Jim Schultz. Jim acted in more of

California State University Archives

The 1971 Cal State Fullerton Cross Country Team

an advisory role than anything else. We would tell him how we wanted to train that upcoming week, he would provide insights and help us put our week's training together, and we were ready to go. Like all athlete-coach relationships, we had times where we got along and times that we didn't, but Jim rarely ever told us to slow down or stop putting in the work. Plus, he always got us to the meets he promised we'd go to, whether it was the NCAA or Amateur Athletic Union (AAU) National Championships.

We were also fortunate to have a great head track & field coach in Dr. Ron Witchey. Ron was an outstanding multi-event coach who worked with multiple All-Americans at Fullerton as well as California State Champions later in his career, when he went on to coach at Santa Ana Junior College. Ron continuously worked as a go-between for the cross country team and Jim when things got too difficult for us to handle. He also was an academic advisor at Fullerton and made sure we got academic help when needed.

When the guys on the team heard about The Streak, they respected that I was consistent, but also thought I was a nut, which was not atypical when people heard about it—back then, anyway. They even used to joke about tying me up to make sure I didn't go out on certain days, but understood it was a part of my mental framework and that the consistency helped make me the runner I was. The Streak itself continued to make me feel tough and confident; I was still running big miles at a high intensity.

During that first cross country season, our team quickly saw the benefits of our training when we consistently won against many Southern California Division I schools. Personally, I'd had a strong season leading up to our conference championship, which was hosted on the Fullerton campus. Our team had seen enough success that year to attract the attention of *Sports Illustrated Magazine* (when they used to cover cross country), who came onto campus and took pictures of the meet. Although I competed hard that day, I ended taking my first individual loss of the season, finishing third overall. I never handled defeat well, and it especially pissed me off to lose on my own campus in front of the press during a meet I felt I should have won.

After my cool-down, while the team received its award for winning the team title, I went directly to my car and drove to Burbank. I was disgusted with the result of that race and had no desire to celebrate. After a few days of running on my own, I still hadn't calmed down (as I said before, I didn't handle losing that well, especially when I had put in great effort). To add insult to injury, at practice the following Monday, the guys gave me an ample amount of shit for not winning at home and needing time alone. That made my blood boil even more. I didn't wallow in my own self-pity for much longer after that first practice; I knew I would have a chance at redemption during the NCAA Championships.

PULL-OUT SOFA BEDS, BBQ, AND WIND

The 1970 NCAA Division II National Cross Country Championships took place in Wheaton, Illinois, located about fifty miles from Chicago and twenty miles from where I was born in Aurora. The school didn't have the money to put us up in hotels, so we ended up staying with my relatives in various places around town, sleeping on roll-away beds in their basements. And rather than go to fancy dinner banquets like teams do now the night before meets, we had barbeque each night.

Someone who was nice enough to have us as guests was my aunt, Leona Covert. Leona had received a bachelor of science degree in physical education from the University of Iowa and upon moving to Aurora, became one of Illinois's most influential figures in women's athletics. While teaching physical education at West Aurora High, she also acted as the recreation director for the Illinois Department of Corrections School for Girls, the city's playground department supervisor, and the director of crafts. She represented the state for the president's council on lifetime sports and coached cheerleading, basketball, softball, cross country, and track—starting many of those programs herself. She also played a leading role in the implementation of Title IX in 1972, and was eventually inducted into the Illinois Athletics Hall of Fame for her lifetime of service. An avid track and field fan, she would send me the program from the Drake Relays each year, which she attended every year for nearly forty years. She even traveled by car to the 1972 Olympic Trials in Eugene, Oregon, where she watched me participate in the marathon. As much as the guys on our team accomplished in college and beyond, it paled in comparison to what we she did during her ninety-one years on this earth.

The conditions at the Chicago Country Club, which had been the location for the championship for twelve years running, were cold, windy, and tough—just the way I liked it. On a day during which we never saw the sun and with a wind chill of minus two degrees, most of the guys on the team wore gloves and hats, while I chose to do neither. What I did do was cover my entire body in sports balm, which is normally used to help warm up sore muscles. Although the balm turned my skin pink and burned for a few minutes after putting it on, it helped put me in the right physical and mental frame of mind when I began to warm up.

There were unlimited entries into the nationals back in those days, so the field was large at around 350 competitors (again, much different from how championship races are put together today). The first half mile of the race, which was on a gradual uphill (the only portion of the course that wasn't flat), went out very fast, with the lead pack coming through in 2:10. Ron Stonitch, the previous year's champion from Charles William Post College, part of Long Island University, took an early lead, and as he broke away from the field at the halfway mark, I was able to stay right with him. At that point it was he and I racing for the individual championship. Unbeknownst to Ron, he provided some extra motivation on race day with some comments he'd made a few months earlier at the Olympic training camp in Pullman, Washington.

Ron, myself, and thirty of the best professional and collegiate athletes in America had been able to train together for three weeks at Washington State University at the same camp in which I'd first met Gerry Lindgren. When I met Ron, he had asked where I was going to be attending school the upcoming fall, which was to be my first at Fullerton. Upon finding out that I was staying on the West Coast, he laughed and said he "never really worried" about guys from the west beating him, "because the weather would take care of us." That statement combined with my loss from weeks before fueled my fire during the second half of the race.

In the last 800 meters, with the non-stop, frigid wind slapping us right in our faces, Ron was no longer in contention and it came down to me and John Cragg, who ran for St. John's College in Minnesota. During the last 200 meters, John and I were still together. As we sprinted down the home stretch, he took what seemed to be an off-balanced step, and I immediately took advantage of his loss of focus, surged to the lead, and won the race by five seconds.

Ron ended up finishing sixth.

Our team finished second overall, trailing the champions, Eastern Michigan University, by twenty-four points. That win was a confirmation of everything I had worked on for the last three years. Less than 1,000 days after being offered a parking pass as a scholarship, I had gained more confidence than I ever thought I could and was the NCAA Division II Cross Country Champion. (Plus, I'd never missed a day of training to boot.) And although becoming a National Champion was an amazing feat, it paled in comparison to the series of events that would take place over the next two weeks.

CONTINUING TO ROLL

During those days, if you finished in the top fifteen at the Division II Cross Country Championship, you automatically qualified for the Division I Championship the following week. After returning to Fullerton the day after the race in Chicago, I was quickly on another plane to Williamsburg, Virginia, with my teammate Tim Tubb. Although I didn't win the Division I meet, I ended up finishing sixteenth overall, just ten seconds from Marty Liquori (the second high schooler ever to break four minutes in the mile) who finished eighth, and forty seconds off the winner—the great Steve Prefontaine. My sixteenth-place finish was the first Division I All-American honor ever won by a student at Fullerton. Tim didn't run as well as he had at the Division II meet, but we still had one more meet to go in the season—and as fun as the last two meets had been, nothing could compare to what was in store the following week.

The day after the Division I race, Tim and I flew back to Chicago to compete for the Pacific Coast Club in the AAU National Team Cross Country Championships. Just being a part of that team was a great honor, as they were the defending National Champions.

Me and Tim Tubb

The day of the AAU national race was another frigid one in the Midwest, complete with heavy rain. Still, Tim and I were both excited to run with and against many then and future Olympians. The biggest challenge came from the Florida Track Club, whose team included future Olympic Gold Medalist in the Marathon Frank Shorter, and multiple-time Olympian Jack Bachelor. Since Tim and

I had just been added to the team, they didn't have jerseys for us, so, during our first two championship races that month, we ran in the T-shirts and shorts we had warmed up in. I ended up finishing thirteenth as the third man for the club, while Tim ran a fantastic race, finishing as our fifth man and last scorer. The following month, on the cover of *Track and Field News* was a picture of the Florida Track Club standing at the finish line, thinking they had won the meet. But sadly (for them), we had won by three points.

Within a span of five weeks, I went from losing in the Conference Championship on my home course to winning the Division II Cross Country Championship, becoming a Division I All-American (the first in the history of California State University, Fullerton) and being a part of the AAU National Club Championship team. It was truly an incredible time for me.

It was during my time at Valley and the first year at Fullerton that I learned how to become, and then became, my best self. Although the high miles and the hard work played an important part in my success, I learned the value of eliminating excuses, focusing on the task at hand, and increasing my level of commitment so I could achieve my goals. When each day was over, I could look at myself in the mirror and know that if I'd done those three things, whether I'd won the race or not, I could be satisfied with the result—even if the act of losing was something I still hated. And as I moved on to the rest of my career at Fullerton, the skills I'd learned continued to take me places I had never thought possible.

PART III
LUNAR LANDING

TIME FRAME: January 1, 1971 – July 9, 1972
TOTAL DAYS RUN CONSECUTIVELY: 1,447
TOTAL CAREER MILES RUN: 23,273
BIGGEST MILEAGE MONTH: 701
TOTAL CAREER DISTANCE COVERED:
409,604.8 football fields
HISTORY:
- Watergate Scandal
- The L.A. Lakers win thirty-three straight games
- Nixon visits China
- Hank Aaron becomes the first baseball player to sign a contract over $200,000
- *The Godfather* is released in theaters
- On July 21, 1972, fifty-seven murders take place in New York City in twenty-four hours

I ran every day.

"SEE YOU AT HOME"

The 1971 track season at Fullerton began as successfully as the cross country season had concluded. Training was going well and I was racing as fast as I ever had, setting a personal best of 28:08 for six-miles in early February at the Long Beach Relays. But just a week after that, I came down with the flu, transforming my fit body into an aching, coughing, sneezing mess. And to make things worse, this flu lasted as long as any illness I had ever come down with. This sent my sleep, training, and overall life quality right into the tank. I was soon getting crushed by people I would normally beat easily.

I decided to head home to Burbank for a few days and catch up on some rest, eat some home-cooked meals, and hope that the comforting surroundings would revitalize my season. Because of our family's relationship with toughness, you didn't bring up being sick until you were *really* sick. Once Mom concluded you were ill enough to have to miss school or work, both she and Dad did everything they could to rush you back to health. During this bout of illness however, Dad's remedies wouldn't involve hot soup or bed rest.

After being home for a few days, I had begun to feel slightly better, but still felt horrible. And that Saturday morning, I did something I hadn't done in nearly four years—I didn't go run. Dad came home after working a full day at the store and asked me if I had run yet. When I told him no, he did his best to convince me that a jog around Griffith Park would make me feel better. I didn't believe him, but when Dad said you were going to do something, you did it.

Once we arrived and I started to jog around, I didn't feel much better. Along with my fever, I coughed so hard it made my back seize up about every 100 meters. It was a particularly hot spring day, and while attempting to keep my run mostly in the shade of the trees so I didn't pass out, I heard a car start up. When I turned my head to see who it was, I saw my Dad backing out of his parking space.

He then shifted the car into drive and began to pull away.

I bolted toward the car like a bat out of hell, screaming at him to come back. As he drove away, he stuck his hand out the window, waved, and yelled, "See you at home!"

The run back to the house was as fun as you could imagine. It didn't even feel like a run; more so like a long, slow death march through the hot asphalt streets of Burbank. Upon returning home, I was in shock. Once I staggered back inside and saw Dad cozied up on the couch with his cigar, it was hard for me to get any words out, not only because I felt like I was going to die, but due to the state of astonishment I experienced after he had basically left me for dead. When I asked him why he would do something like that, his response, as usual, was exactly what I needed to hear: "Look, Mark, you have races you need to train for. Just because you're sick, there's no reason you need to take a day off."

After that day, I don't think I complained or thought about giving up on anything—running or otherwise—ever again.

The illness went on for quite some time after. After finishing fifth in the three-mile and dead last in the mile at our Conference Championship, and with the National Championships just two weeks away, I knew something would have to change with my health or my state of mind—and quickly—if I was going to show up to the year's biggest meet and not get laughed out of the stadium. Luckily, the team was given a small break and I was able to go home, get some more rest, and fit in a couple of confidence-building workouts with Tabori. This combined with the experience I'd had with Dad a few weeks prior put me in the emotional, physical, and mental frame of mind for the most important meets of the year.

> QUESTION: Has there ever been a time when someone challenged you to do something that, even though you may have not been in the best emotional, mental, or physical place, made you better after it was over?

The Streak continued, and while competing at the University of California, Irvine, soon after I'd recovered, I finally ran a race that wasn't an embarrassment. At the National Championship a week later, I finished third in the six-mile final, hanging in there until the last few laps. The following night, I was third in the three-mile, which I was happy with, knowing I didn't have (and never had) the best leg speed.

To say I had transformed my season was a bit of an understatement.

Like cross country, if you finished in the top seven at the Division II Track Championship, you qualified for the Division I meet the following week. Due to my lack of speed, I didn't expect to place very high at the championships, which were located in Seattle. Still, just like always, I planned to push to the front and to make it a tough guys' race. My strategy worked great until the last 800 meters, where my lack of turnover, along with having raced six times in the last three weeks, finally caught up with me, resulting in a tenth-place finish.

A week later at the AAU Championships (now known as the USATF Championships) in Eugene, Oregon, I was entered again in the six-mile, this time running for the California Track Club. I relied on my ability to concentrate. So, against many of the professionals I'd seen at the cross country championships in the fall, and Division I runners I'd competed against the week prior, I ended up finishing tenth. Not bad considering I beat many of the guys who had kicked my ass when I was sick or the week before at the Division I meet. I was pleased to end my season the way I did. My success wasn't just a testament to the number of miles I had put in, or the continued boosts The Streak gave my confidence. My results stemmed from my ability **to persevere and be resourceful.**

I define perseverance as **staying focused and continually making strides toward a goal, no matter what obstacles or even failures you may encounter.** The road to success is paved with failure. So, examine your roadmap and make the needed adjustments to where you *want* to go, and where you *need* to go. You may have just a matter of moments to determine your plan for perseverance, but when you make the decision to come out and face the music, you are granted a space in which you can reveal who you are and who you can become. And although perseverance is vital to both long- and short-term success, having the resourcefulness to adapt to a constantly changing environment helps creates opportunity in situations that seem hopeless.

NOBODY CARES ABOUT SEPTEMBER

Many people believe perseverance, just like toughness, can't be trained. Or they believe perseverance is an inborn talent only found in those who are naturally strong-minded or strong-willed.

That's a lie.

I know perseverance can be trained because I've coached athletes who sat on bus rides home after a meet, holding their heads in their hands for hours, crying the entire way back to campus when things didn't go their way. But the next day after their tears had dried, we talked, created a plan, and worked together to come back from failure.

During The Streak, I often wasn't sure how to deal with losing a championship, or getting injured or sick. So I created plans that kept me moving, training, and putting one foot in front of the other. It was those plans, along with my commitment to them, that got me through each day, not just when I was competing, but in all aspects of my life.

Don't wait until you start to falter to focus on perseverance or to carefully examine your plans. It's a constant state of being. Whether you are up by thirty seconds in your league cross country championship or two days behind in your work, you should always put in the same effort. Those who consistently exist in a state of noteworthy effort, heightened self-awareness, and personal examination are the first ones to reach where they want to be.

During my time at L.A. Valley, as I mentioned before, our biggest rival in Southern California was Pasadena City College. They were a gritty, no-bullshit group of guys who, when they beat you, would always rub it in your face. And when they saw you again, they made sure you remembered what had happened at the last meet. It was the type of effort that made us hate them on the course, but we respect them for it. At the very first meet I ran at L.A. Valley College (after a summer of training during which I'd run over 2,000 miles), we beat Pasadena for the first time ever. What made that win especially rewarding was that Pasadena was in the middle of a string of conference and state championships, making any win against them, by any team, a major accomplishment.

After our victory, we were very excited, just as the guys from Pasadena would be when they beat us several weeks later. (Like I said, we had some battles between our two teams. That's what made the rivalry so much fun. We would win some, they would win some.) While we celebrated, Jesse Gomez, the leader of that era's Pasadena team and one of the toughest people I'd ever come across both in athletics and in general, made his way across the finish chute after reading the results. It was clear he wanted to say something to me and as we stepped closer to one another, we stuck out our hands and shook with the firmness and honesty of two warriors whose respect for one another could not be greater.

At first Jesse kept it short, saying, "You ran really well, Mark." But as we continued to shake, his grip tightened, he pulled me in closer, and with a tug of my arm and a stone-cold stare, he made it clear that he hadn't come over just to wish me a good job. Although Jesse was short and unassuming in his figure, I knew he didn't take any shit. I thought he might take a swing.

"Remember one thing," he added. "No one will remember a Goddamn thing about who won today—some shitty little meet in September. What people remember is what happens in November at the last race of the year. So, enjoy this as much as you want, but at the end of the year," he concluded, squeezing the crap out of my hand, "we are gonna be at the state meet—and I'm gonna kick your ass."

Jesse released his grip, turned, and jogged away. Then, as if he were a prophet, they went on to kick the living shit out of us for the rest of the season … until the Regional and the State Cross Country Championships—where we crushed Pasadena.

Jesse and I shook hands at the state meet too. I had just won my first State Cross Country Championship as an individual, and L.A. Valley had won its first team championship. Jesse and I have remained great friends ever since those days. He went on to coach track and cross country at Pasadena for many years after, with teams that had the same heart, determination, and grit Jesse used to have when he competed.

Success, although it can act as a great validator of the work you've done, should also act as a reminder that the work needs to continue. **Moments are fleeting.** Don't let winning make you too comfortable.

Yeah, we'd beat Pasadena and were excited about it, but just because we'd had one good race didn't guarantee we'd win when we were handed shit during the rest of the season. Each win had to be earned. Every victory had to be paid for with miles of training, and losses that taught us how to better ourselves.

1971 Team reunion

Perseverance is strongly affiliated with memory. After you achieve success, it's easy to forget all the hard work you put in, as well as the struggles and losses you experienced along the way. But be careful, that forgetfulness can bite you in the ass. If you don't put in the work every single time, failure can overtake your joy of past accomplishments in just a matter of seconds. Continued fortitude, no matter the outcome, is at the heart of perseverance. Those who decide they're something special after just one victory are at risk for becoming one hit wonders.

When Jesse made those comments to me, it was the best motivator anyone could have provided at that point in my life. Why? Well, because Pasadena continued to kick our asses ... until the regional and state meets.

Then, we won.

> QUESTION: Was there a time in your life where you basked too much in your own successes and stopped persevering? How did that affect your success for the next challenge?

As the years of The Streak continued to pile on, I consistently worked to improve. If I lost a race, especially when I was really pissed off, I went back out the next day and kept training. When I won, I still laced up my shoes and ran the next day. I refused to settle or become complacent. There was always another race to prepare for and another challenge in front of me.

The morning after the 1971 national track championships at Fullerton, as some of the guys from North Dakota State were getting in their vans to head back home, they saw me out early in the morning as I was finishing my run. Someone shouted at me and asked why I wasn't taking it easy. After all, the season was over. I yelled back at them:

"I know. But cross country season started today."

"I think teams at [California State University] Fullerton were successful because of two things. First, there was no 'hard day, easy day,' training on those teams. Not only were most of us running between eighteen and twenty miles a day, the majority of our runs were extremely intense. And the group was so competitive, you didn't want to be the last guy in after a run or someone was going to give you a hard time. So, even when you felt bad, you still did what you could to save face. Secondly, those teams ate, slept, and breathed running. We went to class and we ran. Nothing else really mattered to us that much. We were a team that was completely obsessed with winning a national championship. When we were not in class, winning that meet was something we thought about every minute of every day. And Mark was the leader of our group. He was my roommate, and several times I heard him get up at 2:30 a.m. He would put his gear on to go run, head out the door, and come back a few minutes later. Turns out he was sleep walking. Even when he dreamed, he thought about running. That is how engrossed his mind was in wanting to be successful."

Dave White
First high school athlete in Orange County
California to break 9:00 for two-miles
2 x All-American in cross country and track at
California State University, Fullerton
1973 AAU National Champion—One-hour run
1972 Olympic Trials Participant—Marathon

ANOTHER SHOT

During the 1971 cross country season, we had all the same guys on the team who'd helped us become the runner-ups in '70. We added to that Chris Hoffman, who came into Fullerton as the only person in the history of the California Interscholastic Federation to win three consecutive individual Southern California Cross Country Championships. As a result, we beat up on everyone we faced no matter what division they were in, including a big win in Sacramento against Division I powerhouse Stanford right before championship season. We swept our conference championships that year when we crossed the line as a group and took the top six places. However, as the national championship approached, I started to come down with yet another cold. And by the time we returned to Wheaton with another opportunity for a team title and for myself to repeat as champion, I was officially sick.

Our routine the week leading up to the championship was identical to the one the year before. We all returned to roll-away beds in my relatives' basements in Illinois, and our nightly cookouts of burgers and steak acted as our staple diets before we returned to the Chicago Country Club for a chance at redemption.

The weather was much different than the previous year—mid-50s, sun shining bright, and no wind. Gone was the punishing wind and frigid cold that made it a tough man's race the year before. Present however was my nagging cough and stuffy nose. Still, I wasn't planning on phoning it in. I was in great shape, had a team around me that was on a mission, and was still ready to get after it.

Just as if someone had pulled a page straight from the script of the previous year's competition, the start of the race was fast as hell. Tim Tubb, Mike Slack from North Dakota State, and I broke away from the field early. Right before the four-mile mark, with the three of us in a group, Mike did something I hadn't seen all year. As we came around a big turn that was thick with grass, Mike began to drive his arms aggressively and turn his legs over at a simply astounding rate—without seeming to labor at all. Within a few seconds, our pack of three had been disbanded, as Mike was quickly up by yards. It was a moment I still think about with amazement. He was able to move with such aggression and power, and I, trying to find identical strength, was unable to. It wasn't that my tank was empty—I just couldn't replicate his movement. While he turned over like a well-oiled machine, I felt as if my legs couldn't switch gears. I was so focused on Mike's move, I didn't notice Tim as he quickly responded to the move with a burst of his own. By the time I came to my senses, they had both gotten away from me. In the final half mile, I began to close the gap on Tim, but it was too late to make the push I'd need to repeat as National Champion. I finished third overall.

As we all stood in the finishing chute, newly crowned Champion Mike Slack came over and boasted that his North Dakota State team had captured the team title, with three guys in the top seven places.

"That's great," Tim told him with a smile on his face, "but we got four in the top nine."

That quieted Mike real quick.

And after Dave White finished fortieth, Fullerton became the 1971 NCAA Division II Cross Country Team Champion.

To be honest, I was disappointed I didn't repeat as individual champion. I was in such great shape, I thought I could win it again, although no defending champion ever had before in Division II. But I just couldn't overcome getting sick and not being able to respond to Mike's aggressive move. Somedays you have it, somedays you don't. Mike and Tim had it that day, and I just didn't.

It was, however, vindicating as a team to win after losing the year before. It was particularly special for the group of us who had all entered school at the same time; we were mostly junior college athletes who hadn't been heavily recruited. And what it proved to each of us was that all the days of challenging each other at practice, of waking up before the sun came up to go on long runs through the orange groves, and all the personal sacrifices we had made—were worth every single step.

With my illness still lingering, I should have pulled the plug on my season after the race I ran the following week at the Division I Championships. I finished fortieth—twenty-five places behind where I'd finished the previous year. But I kept competing and raced at the AAU National Championships that were in San Diego that year—and it was a disaster. I finished in the sixties and honestly, although I was happy the season had ended, I never lost sight of the next challenge down the road. I dusted myself off, and took a few weeks to get healthy. Although track season was a few months away, I had another challenge in mind that I wanted to take on.

STARTING AGAIN

After finishing third at the '71 Cross Country Championships, failing to repeat as champion, and having two less-than-ideal meets immediately after, I took it easy, simply jogging around and trying to get myself back to a place where I could train illness-free. Once I got healthy, I decided to do something both my coaches and teammates thought was crazy: rather than compete in the 1972 track season for Fullerton, I would red-shirt, and focus on training for—and hopefully making—the 1972 Olympic Team in the 10,000 meters. Having finished in the top ten in the six-mile AAU National Championships, and not knowing where life would lead me by the time the '76 trials rolled around, I felt this was the ideal time to try to make the Olympic team. Of the thirty or so people who would qualify for the Olympic trials in each individual event, about three-quarters of them were just happy to participate. And although qualifying was and is an outstanding accomplishment, I didn't want to be someone who was content with just qualifying; I wanted to represent my country at the Olympics. Still, I didn't feel I could train at the level I needed to while going to school full-time and racing a full track season. After telling Coach Schultz and Coach Witchey my plan, I dropped my credits down to part-time status, moved back in with my parents, and returned to training with Tabori.

I then began a routine that only took place two days a week, but was incredibly challenging. On Monday and Wednesday mornings at 5:30 a.m., I would leave the house in Burbank by 6:00 a.m. and make the one-hour drive to

Fullerton, where I would take two classes, then drive back home immediately after with hopes of squeezing in a quick nap before practice started in the early evening. Between juggling my time and concentrating my efforts on both school and training, this routine was physically challenging due to my high training volume, it was mentally draining due to the lack of quality sleep, and it was an emotional test with each day seeming more challenging than the next. I'd train with Tabori on the track for a few hours a night, I'd sit in the car for a few hours a day, and then I'd try to study and get a decent night's sleep—it was almost impossible. And when I decided to jump into a few meets to see how I was doing, the results were nothing short of appalling.

After dropping out of a 5K at California State, Los Angeles, in the middle of the spring, I made the difficult decision to break away from Tabori. As much as I respected him and was grateful for all the time he had put in with me both then and at Valley, the constant pounding on the track was just no longer working for me. Our split from one another was not as peaceful as I would have liked. He was pissed I was going out to train on my own and when I told him I was leaving, we both said some things we shouldn't have (things that are too colorful to repeat here). We ended up not talking for almost a year. When we eventually made our peace many years later, we agreed we should have dealt with our split more professionally.

We've remained close ever since.

LEARNING TO BECOME RESOURCEFUL

After my split with Tabori in the spring of '72, I was left to train on my own for the first time in my life. Training solo wasn't as simple as just heading out the door each morning and figuring out what I would do that day. Due to a high level of self-awareness and situational awareness, however, I was able to read my body effectively, feed it what it needed when it needed it, and use what I had learned from training more than 20,000 miles over the last few years to my advantage. If I needed to go easier, I did. If I felt as if I was ready to train hard for a few days, I pushed without hesitation. I had no one telling me what to do; the responsibility was all my own.

It was liberating.

However, **I quickly realized that in your quest to achieve your goals, if things don't go the way you want them to, resourcefulness can be even more important than training right or having the perfect coach. Resourcefulness isn't just about utilizing all the tools you have at your disposal. It's about re-assessing your situation, forging a new plan, and creating a road you can still run on.**

Some of us (hell, most of us), don't have all the resources we desire. We do, however, have the resources we *need* to make amazing things happen in our lives. While many fail because they are stuck in their ways of thinking, those who are willing to be innovative during their journey are those who can look back years after they've concluded their trek and have no regrets.

One critical step toward becoming more resourceful is learning not to judge yourself. At this point in my career, I was a terrible judge of how I was doing as an athlete when results didn't go my way. Although I would keep training after a loss, it would always fluster me easily (which is something my father was never happy about). And after going through a training and racing experience with Tabori that had produced less-than-desired results, the voice in my head, once filled with confidence, was now telling me how much I sucked. The worst part about it wasn't necessarily the voice itself—it was the fact I listened to it.

Once I was able to calm my mind and skim through the haze of negativity and disappointment, something became clear to me that would be important not just when it came to running, but in my life for years to come. At that current moment, as an athlete, did my performance and training suck? Yes, it did. But that didn't mean I, as a runner or as a person, sucked. And just because I was in a rut rather than a groove, that didn't mean I was never going to be successful again. I just needed to stop judging and begin observing.

> QUESTION: Do you judge your performance or observe it? What are things you can change to become more of an observer of your own performance rather than someone who judges it?

As we grow up, everyone is told not to judge others. It's rude, it's disrespectful, and it doesn't give you a chance to find out who that person really is. But the same goes when examining yourself. If you're taught to treat others with respect, you should do the same with your own thoughts and actions. When we don't perform well and we judge ourselves, phrases like these always seem to pop up in our vocabulary:

"I suck."

"I'm terrible at this."

"I'm never going to be worth a damn."

Not only is judging yourself nonsensical, but it says something about how you are acting in that moment. (Judging yourself also is negative self-talk, which is unhelpful to positive performance). In moments of self-judgment, which usually take place while we are failing or after we have failed, we don't see things how they really are.

You don't suck—but the feeling after a loss does.

You are not terrible—you may just need more work.

You *always are* **worth a damn**—you may just need to have more patience.

Every time I failed, especially as I got older and understood the importance of reflection and observation, I took it as an opportunity to look back at my journal, talk to my coaches and teammates, and take time to think about what I needed to do so I could adjust my training, re-adjust my lifestyle, and set new short- and long-term goals.

In the real word, losing happens. You will lose all the time. Maybe the grade you got was less than you wanted, the route to the field was blocked off so you were late to practice, or the dinner you cooked for your family tastes like horse dung. Successful people understand these types of things happen. They know perfect days rarely happen, but there is always a *chance* for perfection depending on your level of **effort,** your **toughness,** and your **commitment** to getting up after you have been knocked down.

Let's talk about how resourcefulness and observation are connected. Without the willingness to observe rather than judge, you will never be in the mental or emotional space to use the tools at your disposal. Bitching, moaning, and telling yourself how shitty you are does nothing but block the pathways toward growth. It's impossible to utilize your coaches' advice, relish the encouraging words of your loved ones, or remain emotionally open to any new routes of preparation if you judge who you are and how you perform. Just take a deep breath, come back to earth, and find a way—because there always is one.

QUALIFYING

After I stepped away from daily track workouts and spent a few weeks upping my mileage, I entered the World Masters Marathon in Orange, California, which started and finished on the track at Chapman College. Though the 10K was my strong suit, I felt I at least I had a chance at qualifying in the Marathon. After a race where I felt I did ok, but not great (finishing fifth overall), I qualified for the trials. However, it was my Fullerton teammate Dave White who took the title that day. This wasn't a big shock to me because although I was in excellent shape, Dave and my other teammate, Doug Schmink, were big proponents of doing twenty- to twenty-two-mile runs on the weekend, which I had never been a fan of. Running sixteen to eighteen miles hard was something I enjoyed much more. After some reflection, I realized that not doing those long runs was a major gap in my training. Dave's and Doug's commitment to long runs made them much stronger in the Marathon than I was.

Doug, Dave, and I would make history later that year when each of us were ranked in the top ten in the country in the Marathon; we were the only three athletes from the same collegiate team to ever accomplish this. No other group has done it since. (Schmink would also go on to be America's youngest national marathon champion a year later. Never again until Ryan Shea won the Marathon National Championships over thirty years later did someone that young win the title). And although I qualified for the trials in the Marathon that day, the 10K was still my primary focus, where I felt I had the strongest chance to make the Olympic Team.

That dream didn't last very long.

I simply couldn't get things going on the track that spring the way I wanted. Looking back, it was probably a combination of lots of miles and not being the right 10k race that assisted in making the decision to go with the Marathon at the trials in '72. Oddly enough, however, the trials race wouldn't just take me to Eugene, Oregon—but to the surface of the moon.

"LIKE NOTHING YOU HAVE EVER SEEN BEFORE"

The 1972 Olympic Trials saw one of the most unique and talented group of athletes the nation's track community had ever compiled. Jim Ryan attempted to make his third team in the 1,500m, eighteen-year-old high schooler Dwight

Stones was on his way to making his first of three teams in the High Jump, and future 800m Olympic Champion Dave Wottle would break the world record for that event on the second-to-last day of the meet. This was also the meet most University of Oregon track fans had been waiting four years for—as it was the opportunity for Steve Prefontaine, the most charismatic and popular distance runner America had ever seen, to make his first Olympic Team in the 5,000 meters.

What Yankee Stadium is to baseball, Heyward Field is to track and field. In no other venue was there as a great fan base, as electric an atmosphere, and / or a setting as pristine as Eugene, Oregon, during a late-afternoon track meet. As someone who had been there the year before to compete at the AAU National Championships, I knew all too well how exciting it could be to race in that environment. And back then, with no world championships, the Olympics meant everything not just to one's momentary success—but to the solidifying of one's legacy. It was at Heyward Field where runners, throwers, and jumpers went on to become icons.

I called the dorms at Oregon home for ten days before the start of the marathon. Several of us who knew each other worked out on the track each day and just as if we were simply spectators, saw nearly every event. I used this time to get my mind off what I needed to accomplish that week, while soaking in a once-in-a-lifetime experience.

One afternoon, word spread around the track that a small running store called Blue Ribbon Sports in downtown Eugene was giving away free T-shirts. Being someone who could always use free running gear, I hustled down to the shop and discovered it was not much more than a hole-in-the-wall. It really didn't have much to it other than a few running posters, some cheap shirts, and a handful of shoes for sale. But adding to the décor that afternoon were athletes standing wall-to-wall, all looking to get their free shirts. (You've got to remember that in 1972, with no such thing as "professional" track athletes back then, we didn't make anything when it came to sponsorships. So, anything both legal and free was a huge deal.) With the fashion of the time being big hair and big mustaches, the crowd at the store looked more like the audience of a Jefferson Airplane concert than runners in a track meet.

As I watched my shirt get pressed with my nickname, "Bushman" (that I got from my long beard and hair that I hadn't cut in about two years), the store's manager, Geoff Hollister, came over and introduced himself. Geoff said he knew who I was from the previous year's national meet. No more than five minutes into the conversation, he'd made a proposition that would change the course of my life.

"Would you be interested in trying something for us?" Geoff asked. "We have a pair of shoes we would love for you to run in. We'll make a tracing of your foot and create a shoe right from that. They'll be like nothing you've ever seen before. It's called the 'Moon Shoe.'"

Without hesitation, I told Geoff I would be happy to take him up on his offer. I took off my shoes and socks, and placed my foot on a piece of white butcher paper where he traced it with a charcoal pencil. He told me to pick them up in two days. Upon returning to the store, Geoff proved to be true to his word. The shoes he put in my hand were like nothing I had ever seen. When I turned them upside down to look at the soles, replacing the flat bottom was something that looked like what a person would wear in a science fiction comic. The soles were covered with raised rubber nubs and the sides included weird a black stripe that Geoff said was called a "swoosh."

"What did you make this out of?" I asked.

"It's a waffle sole material that was put together at the shoe repair store, located next door. The bumps on the bottom are gonna make your legs feel fresher. Rather than having the shock go immediately up your legs, the rubber nubs will take the shock for you. You are going to get halfway through your race and feel like a million bucks compared to what you would feel like if you wore something else."

I told him I would work out in them a few times, then come back to tell him what I thought.

Jordan Geller

Turns out, the shoes were not that bad.

Not only were they as good as any shoe I had previously trained in, but the fact that these had real insoles—which no other running shoe had back then; most simply had a piece of cardboard or thin cloth glued into the sole of the shoe—made them that much more comfortable. When I returned to the store a few days later, I told him I would be happy to race in the shoes, but on one condition: he had to give me one more T-shirt. He didn't object to my proposition.

Little did we know that this deal would lead to a longtime friendship between Geoff and me, secure my place in history, and spark my relationship with Nike Running.

"A FREAK IS GOING TO MAKE THE OLYMPIC TEAM"

Going into the 1972 Olympic Trials in the Marathon, I thought that on the right day with the right set of circumstances, I could make the team. Being ranked around thirtieth going into the meet would mean something to most, but to me, frankly, it didn't mean much. Rankings were not something that predicted the outcome of races. Once we toed the line, everyone was equal in my eyes and anyone could be beat. Being that I was never a *start out in the back and make your way up to the front of the race* kind of guy, I was ready to be just as aggressive and take just as many risks as I had during any other championship race in which I had competed up to that point. I didn't want to maneuver my way through the field, put things to chance, end up finishing tenth, and wonder what would have happened if I had really gone for it. I needed to come in third or better to make the team, and I was determined.

The race itself took place on the final day of the trials, which turned out to be a hot and sunny Sunday mid-afternoon by the time the race began. The temperature hovered around 85 degrees and by race time in the early afternoon, the air felt heavy with Oregon pollen that hung in the air like a dense fog. It was a big day in Eugene. Not only was our race about to begin, but this was the day that Prefontaine would attempt qualify for the Olympic Team in the 5,000m. That day, Prefontaine would outlast two-mile world record holder George Young, as well as Gerry Lindgren, who famously arrived at the track that day wearing his "STOP PRE" T-shirt. Prefontaine would then make his first and, sadly, his only Olympic Team.

Going into the marathon, I assumed at least half the guys ranked in the top ten wouldn't have the type of day they had when they'd qualified. (After all, it required a heroic effort just to get in.) They'd probably had just one great race to qualify, or the course they'd qualified on was flat as a pancake and as fast as a skating rink. I knew not everyone was going to feel perfect that day, either. Several guys would not be able to take the pressure, their negative self-talk would take them out of the race, and if I just could be myself, I would be right there when I needed to be.

Scott Schweitzer, 1972

There was lots of talk leading up to the start of the marathon that it was going to go out fast, but I figured that even if that happened, I was going to go for it anyway. And with the course being mostly flat, if it went quick, there was a good chance it would remain that pace throughout.

It did go out fast.

… But not *too* fast.

By mile five, my predictions were proven correct. A breakaway group had formed that included Yale alumnus Frank Shorter, Oregon great Kenny Moore, and me.

Although we still had twenty-one miles to go, I figured if we could get far enough away from the field, I might be able to steal a spot on the team.

At the halfway mark, our group of three was still together and I was feeling pretty good. Moore and Shorter threw some surges in throughout the course, but I continually responded, and by the time we got to mile eighteen, it was still just the three of us. My legs felt resilient (maybe Geoff Hollister had been right about the moon shoes), and the heat, which took down more than a quarter of the field that day, didn't seem to have too much of a negative effect on me. At this point, it seemed I had a legitimate chance to be on the podium.

The way I competed that day, combined with my long, shaggy hair and beard, made me stand out like a sore thumb. At the twenty-mile mark, we passed a local announcer who was covering the race over local radio. At this point in the race, Moore and Shorter had finally created some distance between me and them, and although the gap between us made it clear I wasn't going to win the race, I was still in a solid third place—the last spot to make the team—with six miles left. As the play-by-play analyst noticed this, he uttered something that summed up what everyone was thinking, "Oh, my God. A freak is going to make the Olympic Team."

RETURNING FROM THE MOON

From mile twenty-one to mile twenty-two, as good as I had been feeling, I finally went through a bad stretch. As much as I tried my damnedest to stay in the moment and concentrate, my legs began to lack the turnover they needed to stay in contention.

By the end of mile twenty-two, both Jeff Galloway and Jack Bachelor had passed me and moved away, and, in a matter of minutes, it became clear I wasn't going to make the team. I felt sorry for myself for just a few seconds before I reassessed my situation and realized that just because I wasn't going to make the team didn't mean I shouldn't compete. It was not just a matter of pride that kept me putting one foot in front of the other, but a matter of resourcefulness *and* finances.

During those days, if you finished in the top seven in your event, the track association would give you two hundred and fifty dollars. That was a hell of a lot of money back then—and I was determined to get paid. So rather than pout for the next six miles, I chose to be resourceful. I used that financial incentive as motivation to keep putting one foot in front of the other, since nothing would come from just going through the motions.

Gregg Brock went on to pass me at mile twenty-three, along with Stanford legend Don Kardong who caught me around mile twenty-four. As I entered Heyward Field for the race's final 400 meters, it was clear that I was going to finish in the top seven and get my money. But as rewarding as my check would be, nothing compared to the reaction I received from the crowed while completing my final lap.

Announcers provided updates to the spectators during the duration of the race, and, oddly, I had become somewhat of a fan favorite. Having been a Division II guy and not ranked in the top fifty of the race before it began, it was clear I was an underdog. As I came around the turn, the crowd rose to their feet, giving me a standing ovation. Having competed in the front of the race for so long, then seeing my Olympic dream disappear so close to the finish line, that brief moment of recognition from the crowd was something I treasured then and still do today.

Geoff Hollister's gamble on giving me the moon shoes also paid off—as I became the first person to cross the finish line in a pair of Nike running shoes. That was a moment that would go down in Nike's history; those shoes were just the beginning of the world's largest sporting-shoe and apparel company. That first pair now rests in a museum in Portland.

Even though I didn't make the team, I did what I'd intended to do: I threw myself into the mix with the contenders and gave it my best shot to make the team. Shorter would go on to become the Olympic Champion in the Marathon a few weeks later and I returned to Fullerton, with one last track season to go before graduation. But I left Eugene with two free T-shirts, a pair of shoes, two hundred and fifty dollars, and a place in history that wasn't bad at all for a guy who'd been offered a parking pass scholarship just four years earlier.

FINAL THOUGHTS ON PERSEVERANCE AND RESOURCEFULNESS

If you focus on what's right in front of you with a fighting attitude and with toughness, then you will be in the best position to obtain your goals.

The challenges you face each day may not be centered around getting your workout in. They could be related to your job, your relationships, or simply remaining committed to being the best version of yourself. As hard as things get, as frustrating as life will be, as many failures as you will eventually face—there is never a reason to automatically throw in the towel. You have the power to change your situation. You have the control to focus on the step that is right in front of you.

None of us know what the future holds for us. When I was in high school, if you had told me I was going to compete in the first pair of Nike Shoes ... well, I would have asked you what the hell a Nike was. But hard work and a bit of luck landed me a place in history. The same can happen for you. Just continue to put one foot in front of the other.

PART IV
ON THE RUN

TIME FRAME: July 10, 1972—July 23, 1976
TOTAL DAYS RUN CONSECUTIVELY: 2,718
TOTAL CAREER MILES RUN: 45,708
TOTAL CAREER DISTANCE COVERED: The equivalent length of 165,982.2 Empire State Buildings
BIGGEST MILEAGE MONTH: 641
HISTORY:

- Average cost of gasoline in the United States hits $0.55
- Bobby Fischer becomes World Chess Champion
- Mark Spitz wins seven gold medals in swimming at the 1972 Olympics
- Terrorists kill eleven at the 1972 Olympics
- HBO launched
- The VW Beetle sells its 15 millionth car, becoming the most popular car ever sold

I ran every day.

SQUARE ONE

Since the beginning of The Streak in the summer of 1968, a time that many considered to be one of the nation's most dividing and chaotic, California State University, Fullerton, had gone from a quiet commuter school nestled among orange groves to a hotbed of political and social activism. Students were still protesting the Vietnam War, defending their rights to free speech, and uniting as a student body against targeted ageism, racism, and sexism by campus faculty, staff, and police. Emotions ran so high at one point that in 1970, multiple university-wide actions, protesting the on-campus appearance of then Governor Ronald Reagan, led to the arrest of forty students and two professors. When I arrived on campus that fall, the chant "pigs off campus," referring to the desire to remove any type of law enforcement on campus, was one that echoed through our university quads on a nearly constant basis. As the world around us continued to evolve, boys my age and younger were being sent off to Vietnam to fight in a war we really didn't understand (and still don't). Meanwhile several of my classmates were imprisoned for exercising their First Amendment rights and desiring a life after college that would lead our country into the next century.

Personally, I had no idea what the future would hold for me other than the fact that I had one track season left and no place to go once it wrapped up. Like with most college seniors, graduation loomed on the horizon, and my life was coming to a crossroads.

My daily runs, however, were the one thing in my life that remained consistent, strong, and allowed me to feel confident in myself. During runs I could focus on something I enjoyed doing, and no matter the chaos of the world, I was provided with peace and security. Running was the thing I looked forward to each day more than anything; nothing could rival the exhilaration I felt when I took that first step each morning. And after my surprising performance at the Olympic Trials, the thought of trying again for the Olympics didn't seem so far out of reach.

Back in the 1970s, NCAA athletes were not given the opportunity to compete once they completed their undergraduate degrees. Once you finished your bachelor's degree, you were done. So, to ensure I could race for the track team in the spring of 1973, I again dropped my credits below full-time status, and turned my attention toward preparation for the upcoming season. After the terrible experience of commuting back and forth from my parents' house the previous spring, I decided to remain at Fullerton that fall to train with the guys. But just when things started to get moving in the right direction with training and the small bit of school I had left, my focus got pulled in an unexpected direction.

THE STORE

Nike was still a very small company, and at the time had no mass distribution operations. Most of their salespeople were selling shoes out of their cars before and after cross country or track meets. As they wanted to expand their client base, their marketing strategy included finding runners that had some name identification to create some buzz for their products. Turned out I was popular enough (at least to them) to be a part of the program. Geoff Hollister contacted me one summer afternoon and asked if I would be interested in becoming the manager of Nike's first Orange County California brick-and-mortar store, the Athletic Department. I said "yes," and few months later I had the keys.

Even before the store opened, the company began sending shoes and shirts to my apartment for me to sell at local high school meets and road races—all out of the trunk of my Plymouth Fury. (I'm confident this marketing strategy would be frowned upon by the NCAA today.)

Having a job did not for one second negatively affect The Streak or my ability to train. In fact, it forced me to create a strict schedule in which I had to create time to attend classes, train, run the store, and sell shoes from my car. And since I'd learned my lesson all too well during my red-shirt season of 1972 about the importance of balance and self-awareness, one thing became incredibly clear: if I was going to make this next season of my life work the way I wanted it to, creating an environment and a system in which I could hold myself accountable was going to be as important as any amount of work, training, or studying

I could do. Furthermore, I learned that holding others accountable is sometimes just as important as holding yourself to the standards you set.

ACCOUNTABILITY

I define accountability as taking responsibility for the commitments you have made. As I have said throughout this book, I never wanted to be someone who made a promise to others or myself and then backed out on it. My journal acted as one accountability system, but I also had my team, my coaches, and my bosses at Nike to keep me in line when it came to running well and being successful in school and business. However, as important as all of those pieces were, there was one key thing, something many people don't talk about, that trumped everything when it came to holding myself accountable. This one little thing helped me head out the door each morning to run, go to school, and go to work: **I cared.**

> QUESTION: What do you do, specifically, on a daily basis to hold you and/or the members of your team accountable?

Nothing, not a damn thing, matters more when it comes to holding yourself and others around you accountable than caring. Caring about something is the difference between going to practice to put in meaningful work and just showing up to go through the motions. It's the difference between studying for ten minutes before an exam and burying your head in a book for hours to make sure you get an A. It's the difference between getting moving and doing nothing. Let's make one thing clear: no one ever did remarkable things by simply sitting on their ass. They had clear goals, understood the path they needed to forge, set standards for themselves and those around them in order to stay on that path, and (most importantly), even if they failed, continued to get up and fight tenaciously to get where they wanted. That is how I looked at training—and my life. I had goals and standards I'd set and I continually examined whether I was doing what needed doing. Not because I needed to, but because I wanted to. Because it mattered to me.

I hope that whatever you are doing, wherever you are in the process toward achievement, it matters to you. If it does, that will make things easier. If it doesn't, you need to ask yourself why that is. If you are not sure, then you really need to ask yourself if it's something you should continue doing.

As the years of The Streak began to pile on, accountability became more and more crucial. I would eventually no longer have a team to train with, I had a new Olympics goal that was only 1,500 days away, and my future promised little to no stability toward my financial or living situation. The only things that were consistent in my life were the joy I received from heading out in the mornings to train, the excitement of challenging myself, and the thrill of attempting to answer the question: How good can I be? And if I hadn't cared, I never would have been able to meet my goals.

Are you willing to hold yourself accountable to become the type of person you want to be?

Are you willing to hold other people's feet to the fire when the time comes?

And how much do you care?

The events of the next few years would challenge my ability to compete as an athlete, remain a part of the business community, and eventually teach others the importance of holding themselves and their teammates responsible for the goals they set out to accomplish. My motivation now ran deeper than the daily results I penned in my journal. It was about getting people to understand my goals and their goals, and making sure things got done.

FRUSTRATION AT FULLERTON

I was fit going into the track season of 1973. This season looked to be different compared to ones in the past, at least on paper, as our track and field team at Fullerton had a legitimate chance to win the National Championship. We had myself and Dave White returning; Jim Feeney, who was the defending national champion in the javelin; one of the country's best 4x400m relays; and a slew of other guys on the team who each had an opportunity earn All-American certificates and score points at the end of the year.

Back then, qualifying for a competition was based purely on your ability to reach a specific mark, with no regional qualifiers or limits for number of entries. If you hit the standard, you were in. And unlike today when the NCAA funds your travel to the Nationals, your institution had to pay for your transportation and lodging per diem. (Hence the reason we slept on cots in my relatives' basements for the cross country championships.)

Fullerton qualified many athletes for the championship that year and we were one of the top teams in Division II. But in the middle of what should have been a season to be celebrated, the school informed us that they wouldn't be sending anyone to attend that year's championship, even if we had qualified. All of us—especially Coach Witchey—were furious. University administration provided no rationale for their decision, and scheduling a meeting with any of the top brass to plead our case was about as possible as scheduling a one-on-one with Moses and the disciples—at the same time.

After a few weeks of bargaining between the administrators and Witchey, the powers that be decided they would pay for us to attend the championship—but only if we won the team title at our conference meet. This, again, we found infuriating. Still, we united as a group and committed that we would do whatever we could to win that weekend. And after a long weekend battle with California Polytechnic State University at San Luis Obispo, on a sunny Saturday afternoon in front of our home crowd, we won our conference meet on the day's last event.

But even after all the deals that had been made, and all the effort we had put in to win the conference, the school informed us forty-eight hours later that they would not be sending anyone to the national track championships.

Coach Witchey resigned immediately.

The whole situation was bullshit. Someone had to hold the administration accountable for their decision. And the following day, during which an attempt to meet with the athletic director failed, it was time to take our efforts to another level.

THE MEETING

After a team meeting one afternoon to talk about our situation, fifteen or twenty of us decided to try once more to speak with the athletic director. We walked right into the office, ignoring his secretary, and when we got inside his office, we discovered one of our guys was already there. Upon seeing so many of us in his office, the director became livid. He was pissed we'd walked past his secretary and even more furious we'd had the audacity to confront him. However, he did agree to a meeting the next day.

We would be ready.

In order to ensure our trip to nationals, we hatched a plan: first, hold the administration accountable for going back on their word and second, do it in a way that embarrassed them as much and as publicly as possible. The second piece of the plan involved mass communication. I took the liberty of calling both the *Orange County Register* and the *Los Angeles Times,* letting them know what was happening, and that they should join us on campus to meet with the administration. They were delighted to be a part of our efforts.

Though our action wasn't as big some of the events that had taken place on campus over the last few years, it was, at least to us, just as important. We didn't think we would end up in prison or thrown off campus, but given the way the administration had acted with many of our classmates, there was still a chance something drastic could take place if the meeting escalated. But no matter what happened, the athletic director needed to be held accountable. Held accountable for not providing legitimate rationale for his decision. Held accountable for failing to speak to us directly. Held accountable for extinguishing our dreams. Held accountable for putting our team in such a horrendous situation that one of the best coaches in the nation chose to resign.

> QUESTION: Was there ever a time during which you held someone accountable who wasn't holding up their end of the bargain?

The athletic director, when he arrived in the classroom where we were to meet, encountered an entire room full of athletes. He was all-business and stern, and got right to business. He immediately established what he called "his standards." According to the director, there were three pieces of criteria that must be met in order to attend nationals: first, you had to have met the national qualifying mark; second, you had to be ranked in the top ten in the country in your specific event; and, lastly, the director had to see the marks for himself, along with the national rankings that proved their legitimacy. After he had created his line in the sand, I asked the director if he was telling the truth, and if he was going to lie again once we showed him what he'd requested. The color on his face went from white to a bright red, looking as if his head might pop right off his neck. With a deep and angry sigh, he said, "yes," and agreed to review the lists of rankings we'd brought with us.

In a flash, I pulled out a sheet that listed everyone who had qualified, slammed it down on his desk as hard as I could, and looked him in the eyes.

"Well, get your checkbook ready, because we're going to Wabash."

The team was as exuberant in that moment as they were in any of the meets we'd won that year. Our athletic director's reaction, however, was not just one of defeat, but of utter shock and embarrassment. We ran right out of the facility to tell Coach Witchey, who was waiting for us at the track to hear how the meeting had gone. He was immediately back on board, excited, and (just like the rest of us) relieved we would have a chance to compete in— and possibly win—a national championship. The next day, we purchased our tickets and hotel rooms, and just a few hours later, we were in the air with a chance to bring home a trophy.

Winning the title, however, would be a bit more difficult than we had imagined.

A FULLERTON FAREWELL

With a new lease on life after a horrific few weeks of dealing with the school administration, many of us felt what we'd gone through made us a team of destiny. The team was focused, Witchey was fired up, I was ready to bookend my collegiate career with another team title, and we as a unit wanted to win that trophy so we could shove it right in the faces of our university administration.

The only way I can describe the track at Wabash College is to compare it to a bad parking lot. It was an all-asphalt track with painted-on lines and cracks running up and down it. Plus, in a meet where I had to run heats of the three-mile and the six-mile final, I was concerned recovery was going to be impossible. But, like always, we did our best to try to focus on what we could control, and at the start of the final day of the four-day meet, we had a twenty-three-point lead.

But things didn't go as planned.

The final day of competition unfortunately started not as a roar, but a thud, and slalomed downhill from there. Our javelin thrower, the defending champion in the event, failed to make the final. Our 4x100m relay, which was favored to be in the top three, didn't come close. In the 400m hurdles, our only athlete in the event failed to make it to the starting line. And as we fell apart, Norfolk State, led by Steve Riddick, who would go on to be one of America's best sprinters in the 1970s, would take the team lead mid-meet and never look back. There was no describing how upset we all were once we realized the meet was out of our grasp as the three-mile final came up that evening.

I approached Coach Witchey and told him that since we were out of the running for the team championship, I didn't want to run the three-mile. I had finished runner up in the six-mile the night before (losing by literally one step) and with the team title out of reach, combined with my legs being dead from running on that disgrace of a track for the last few days, I just wanted to go back home. He understood where I was coming from and was just as pissed off as I was. We went back and forth for a bit about what I should do, but after he told me to just go and make sure I made All-American, I sucked it up and got on the line. I finished in sixth place, ending my collegiate career with seven All-American certificates. The team finished third behind Norfolk State and Lincoln University.

We still received a trophy for our team finish, but in a state of utter disgust over our placing, Coach Witchey slammed the trophy into a trash can before we got to the team bus. No one tried to try to fetch it out.

The next two weekends for me were spent at the Division I and AAU Championships. I was entered in the six-mile in both meets, but due to a combination of my legs being spent from running twelve miles on pavement at Wabash College and the emotional strain we'd been through, I ended up dropping out of both meets. It was a sour ending to a career that included a national team championship, an individual national title, and six other All-American experiences.

I wouldn't return to the Fullerton campus for nearly twenty years.

COACH COVERT

The thought of being a coach had never really entered my mind while I was in college. I was in no-man's land—a place many of us are in far too often—and I honestly didn't know what the hell I was going to do (other than continue to run). I moved back in with my parents, picked up odd jobs here and there, and focused on training for the 1976 Olympic Trials in the Marathon. I wasn't motivated to go out and try to find employment and didn't want to do much else other than train.

But sometimes, life points you toward your destiny.

Before coaching at the NCAA level, John Tansley was the track coach at Glendale Community College. He would later go on to immense success at both California State, Los Angeles, and Long Beach State, becoming Long Beach's first coach after they entered the NCAA competition. We knew each other from my days at L.A. Valley, and upon seeing each other at one of Glendale's winter track meets, we shook hands and he immediately asked what I was up to.

I told him the truth—not much of anything other than training, of course.

"Why don't you come over here and coach the distance runners?" he asked. I said "yes" without hesitation, although I had no idea what coaching entailed other than writing workouts. "One thing I got to tell you though, Mark," he added. "I'm not going to be able to pay you." For whatever reason, I didn't see that as a problem.

When I officially joined the staff the following Monday, there were two things I quickly realized: first, the team was *terrible* and second, I had no idea what I was doing when it came to leading a team of my own. Although I had a degree in physical education, there was an art to coaching as far as putting workouts together, along with a way to effectively communicate with the group—both of which I still needed to discover. I had spent nearly a decade surrounded by phenomenal coaches, but I didn't think I could just replicate what they did and have it work for others like it had for me. When I went around to other coaches and athletes asking what to do, most of them said the same thing—"just have them do what you're doing." But as someone who was still training over 100 miles a week and hadn't missed a day of running since the previous decade, this didn't seem like a bright idea.

I didn't feel comfortable talking about how much I was training or how hard I ran. I understood I was unique in how I trained. Not many eighteen-year-old kids were ready to be thrust into 140-mile weeks with no days off. So, rather than discuss my own training, I spent lots of time discussing many of the principles I have shared in this book, as they were the tools that got me from one day to the next. At the heart of these first conversations was the importance of consistency and, of course, accountability. If these kids wanted to be successful in competition, they had to understand when they took a day off, someone else was training. When they decided to go easy on a day in which they were asked to push themselves, there was, no question about it, a group of people pushing harder who they would eventually have to compete against.

I also spoke at great lengths about how training, not just racing, needed to be important to these student-athletes. I did not believe, nor have I ever believed, that making races the center of your training will make you better.

- Training will make you better.
- Focused practice will make you better.
- Preparation will make you better.

These were foreign thoughts to that first group at Glendale. Training was just something they did in between racing; to them it was a pain in the ass and something they did only to guarantee they could race the following weekend. I felt a new train of thought needed to be introduced for them to be successful when they really wanted to be.

- Being on time to practice mattered.
- Taking workouts seriously mattered.
- Not quitting when they got tired during training *really* mattered.

And although these simple truths were ones I tried to emphasize with each group I worked with over the next forty years, it was this first group from Glendale that helped me realize how vital each component was to success.

> QUESTION: What are the things that matter most in your organization, team, or life?

6:00 A.M.

After going through a good, but not great, first track season at Glendale, I decided to do what I learned was one the most important things you can do as a coach—I recruited my ass off. Glendale was surrounded by high schools packed with remarkable talent, and understanding that discovering talent would be a key determinate to our success in the future, there were weeks I spent more time in the halls of Hoover and Glendale High Schools than I did with my own team. So, rather than sit idly by and watch these kids go to other schools, I used my relationships with coaches I knew and used my experience at the trials to get my foot in the door with recruits. And with a bit of luck and lots of hard work, it started to pay off.

Our first summer practice at Glendale that second year featured a team that looked much different (at least on paper) than what we'd had just a few weeks earlier when the track season had wrapped up. Joining us were the Croad Brothers—Greg and Brad—along with Dave Vanderveen, who all had just graduated from Hoover High School. Jay Rabino and John Frizinati from Crescenta Valley High, and Bobby Thomas, from Glendale High also joined the group on that first morning. Our group went from not having any men break 5:00 in the mile the year before, to a group to where everyone had broken 4:45. (I know those times don't exactly light the world on fire, but compared to where we'd been the previous year, I was thrilled.)

Bobby, on the other hand, was a bit better than everyone else.

Bobby Thomas was a skinny, dark-haired kid from Glendale who attended church every Sunday and was as good a person as any coach would ever want. Although he was a 9:05 two-miler his senior year of high school and a good student, he was not recruited by any four-year institutions. And, because of the strong relationship he had with his parents and his church, going to Glendale Community College was magically (at least for me at the time) the perfect fit. What made Bobby even more interesting is that he, along with all the other guys on the team, had not run much in high school, usually averaging about sixty miles a week or so on a peak week of training. I didn't try to make them 200 mile-per-week guys automatically, but I did make it clear that for them to be successful, they were going to have to adjust their training from both an intensity and volume standpoint. No one objected.

This group is where I started a tradition that lasted with my teams for the next forty years—6 a.m. practice. Look, I know getting up before the sun rises and finishing practice before everyone gets to work is not the most desirable thing to do, especially for college kids. But the weather is almost always nice at that time of day in Southern California, we had great places to train (that were all to ourselves), and it allowed the guys to go about their day and get their second run in at a time that best worked for their schedule. Sure, there were times where our Glendale guys were tired for whatever reason in the morning, but they never complained, they showed up when they were told (because when practice started at 6 a.m., we were already warming up by 6:01), and when they started to see the benefits of their training, those early morning sessions became a part of what made our team unique. And after a summer of training together early in the morning, during which they ran more in three months and trained harder than they had in their entire lives, they had forged a bond with each other that was so strong, they believed very few teams in the state could beat them.

Turned out that they were right.

THE RECORD

The 1974 cross country season at Glendale got off to a roaring start with some big wins and epic battles against Moorpark College, who had been, for quite a long stretch, one of the best teams in the California. Bobby Thomas had separated himself from everyone else as the top individual, going undefeated as we rolled into the State Championship, which took place on the world-famous Mount SAC cross country course.

For those of you who know how challenging the course is at Mount SAC, I don't need to tell you much. But for those of you who have not had the luxury of racing there, let me tell you—that course is *hard*. It has gotten faster over time due to the softening of the turns to fit the increasing number of athletes who run at their invitational each year, but when we went to the state meet in 1974, the four-mile course was just as tough as any place in the world. Starting out with a flat first mile, you made your way up a steep hill, famously known as the "switchbacks," where you weaved in and out through a series of sharp turns, which were engulfed by thick trees. After the cresting the hill, you shot down an even longer hill, across an asphalt air-strip, and up "poop-out hill," which had an incredibly high gradient that felt like a sledgehammer to the legs with an elephant strapped to your back. This was then followed by some more hills, and *another* trip up poop-out, up reservoir hill, and finally finishing with a flat sprint to the finish. It was a course designed for tough people. People who could concentrate and block out the constantly changing gradients. Those who could stay present in the moment and do their job.

Our team at Glendale was built to be tough—especially Bobby Thomas.

Glendale ran in the Small Schools State Junior College Cross Country Championship on a bright Saturday morning at Mount SAC. (The fact there was a "small schools" division, I found insulting and preposterous. This was something I worked hard in helping to successfully abolish years later.) And right from the start, Bobby and the guys took right to the field. They went to the front, setting a pace that was so incredibly challenging that from a spectator's perspective, the race looked like more of a chase than anything else. With each mile, Bobby seemed stronger. Up the switch-backs, down poop-out, up the reservoir. Through each difficult part of the race, Bobby eased through it as if it were a workout. Unlike other guys on the course whose faces strained and legs buckled up the hills, Bobby's legs had pop and he crested the hills without tension. With 100m to go, two things were apparent: our team was going to win the state championship, and Bobby had a chance to break the course record. The crowd, not really focused on the team title as we had it wrapped up early, seemed to follow Bobby more and more with each step. A sea of spectators from across the state flooded to every corner of the course, cheering him on so loudly at some points it was difficult to hear my own voice, screaming at him to run through to the finish line.

Bobby would go on to cross the finish line in 19:19 for a Mount SAC four-mile course record that still stands to this day. From 1,500m Olympic Champion and world record holder Noureddine Morceli of Algeria to Wilhelm Giddabouty of Kenya, many have attempted to beat Bobby's record, and all have failed. His is still one of the great records in American distance running. That win was the cherry-on-top of an incredible day for our Glendale College team. We would go on to become the Small Schools California State Cross Country Champions and do it in a dominating fashion that would not be matched for many years. And in what was my first season coaching cross country, their success made it easier for me to recruit athletes from across Southern California for years to come.

Only I wouldn't be recruiting for Glendale College.

By the end of the cross country season, Coach Tansley and I were no longer seeing eye-to-eye. There's no reason to get into the details of what happened, but let's just say he wanted to do things his way and I wanted to do them another. I resigned just a few days after Glendale won the school's first state cross country title.

Through it all, The Streak was alive and well and I continued to train at a high level with the hopes of making the trials in 1976.

Glendale Community College Archives

YOU WILL WIN MOROCCO

Although I stopped coaching at Glendale, Tansley and I came to an agreement that I could continue to write workouts for Bobby as he prepared for the AAU National Cross Country Championships. He would go on to finish twenty-fifth, a placing that at the time was basically unheard of for a junior college athlete. After his finish there, we began to speak openly about his chances of making the World Junior Cross Country team. To do that, he would have to qualify at the Junior USA Cross Country Championship, in a field that was the best that meet had ever seen. The competition included Ralph Serna, an 8:45 high school two-miler who would become the Division II NCAA Cross Country Champion, and Roy Kissin, who would later be an All-American at Stanford and multiple-time Olympic Trials qualifier at 10,000m. After studying the course and coming up with a race plan we thought was fool-proof, there was a good feeling amongst Bobby, Tansley, and me that this could really happen.

With steeplechase barriers placed throughout the course (something you don't see frequently in the states, but in international competition, it was the norm), Bobby's plan was to get with the leaders until the last barrier, and using his long legs, push off the final hurdle and sprint to the finish. Our goal was not for Bobby to simply make the team that day in San Francisco—but to win the meet, something that no Junior College freshman had done in the twenty-five years of the championship. With 200m left in the race, it was Ralph and Bobby pushing toward the final barrier with a national championship on the other side of the finish line. Bobby was always the kind of athlete who coaches dreamed of training. He always did what was asked, never gave less than one hundred percent, and because he was still such a novice and had not formed strong opinions about training or racing strategy, he responded well to everything we discussed. When he and Ralph approached the final hurdle, Bobby did what he always did—he listened. He jumped with his right foot landing directly on top of the barrier and pushed off with such force, it pushed the hurdle backwards and rocketed

Nino Fisanotti

Bobby Thomas

Bobby into a mad sprint Ralph couldn't respond to. And just like that, Bobby, an unrecruited junior college runner just five months earlier, was the USA Junior National Cross Country Champion. Although it was surprising to most, it wasn't to me. Bobby had put in the work, had the talent, and was willing to put his body through things most others weren't.

His success didn't end there.

Bobby's big win qualified him for the World Junior Cross Country Championships, in Rabat, Morocco. The US sent a fantastic team over and the more Bobby trained, the more I thought he had an opportunity to win the meet. Again, he responded well to being coached. When you told Bobby to do something, he did it. When you attempted to motivate him, it worked. Knowing this, I wanted to find a way to keep him focused and hold him accountable to his goal of becoming a World Champion. One afternoon after practice, I mentioned to him that he should purchase some poster board, and put it in a place where he could see it every morning when he woke up and each night before he shut his eyes. The words on this poster were simple:

YOU WILL WIN MOROCCO.

> QUESTION: What unique things do you do to motivate yourself and hold you and the members of your team accountable?

A week before departing for Africa, Bobby would set the national junior college record for three miles, running

13:30 at Long Beach State. I felt that race, along with our non-stop conversations about our race plan, would give him the confidence to be right in the heat of the race when it mattered.

Well, I was wrong.

Bobby was never in the heat of the race.

Rather, he was twenty seconds ahead of the field, kicking their asses.

Bobby Thomas would become only the second World Junior Cross Country Champion in American history—just three others from the States have won since. The USA would also win the team championship, with a string of titles, three-in-a-row, that has never been matched by American cross country runners.

My time working with Bobby would end shortly after that. He would later go on to attend UCLA and become an All-American in cross country for the Bruins a few years after that race in Morocco. Bobby is now a successful Realtor and resides in Southern California with his family, including his son Phillip, who also ran cross country at Glendale College.

Bobby tried harder than any person I have ever coached. But it wasn't how hard he tried, or how many races he won by more than a football field that had the largest impact on me. It was what I took away from my experience with that entire group of men that deeply affected my running streak and my coaching philosophy for the rest of my life. The guys at Glendale truly cared, they were willing to be held accountable, and they actually wanted to do the work it took to be successful.

"You have to realize how little I understood running when I started with the sport. I didn't have much of an idea of what I was doing or even how I was doing it. But Mark always tried to find new ways to keep me motivated, so I never lost interest or became too overwhelmed with the stresses of training and racing at a prominent level. I was nervous going into the World Junior Cross Country Championship, as I basically considered the top guys in that meet to be god-like and I wasn't very confident I could hang with them for an entire meet. So, in the workouts leading up to the meet, Mark spoke a great deal about visualizing the competition, the course, and the scenarios that could take place throughout the meet. At our last practice before I left for Morocco, I had learned to use visualization so well in training, I literally felt like the race was going on. When practice was over, I asked Mark if I had won the meet. Considering Mark was never big on compliments, when he said, 'maybe,' I felt like it was him telling me I was ready. Ten days later, I was the World Junior Cross Country Champion, only eight months after I hadn't received a single scholarship offer. Mark was the kind of person I needed at that time to get me where I needed to be. Without him, I don't believe I would have had the running career I did."

Bobby Thomas
1974 Junior World Cross Country Champion
1973 California Community College State
  Cross Country Champion
Former National Junior College three-mile record holder
Mount San Antonio College cross country course four-mile
  record holder
Member, Mount San Antonio College Cross Country Hall of Fame

BIG BEAR

After Glendale and I parted ways, I returned immediately to training full-time for the 1976 Olympic Trials in the Marathon. The Streak continued, and with my time suddenly free to focus on running, those morning runs by myself were like reuniting with an old friend. (Maybe we'd seen each other every day, but we hadn't had a nice, long talk in a while.) Having spent the last few months focused on the team and with less than eighteen months before the trials, I felt like I needed a change. I needed something to get me back into the correct frame of mind where training and the daily grind (which I enjoyed) were the only things I was dedicated to. It was in a search for solitude that I came upon a one-room log cabin located in downtown Big Bear, California.

Set 6,500 feet above sea level and one hundred miles from Burbank, Big Bear seemed like the perfect location for marathon training and spartan living. The cabin was just one main room, a bedroom, and a bathroom. No heat, no air conditioning, no carpet. The luxuries I had taken for granted over the last twenty-plus years were gone and if my roommate, Brad Croad, who had graduated college and was looking to train post-collegiately also, and I were going to make the strides in our training we were hoping for, it wouldn't be because we were pampering ourselves too much. Instead, we'd toughen up as we trained at elevation for the next few months.

My experience in Big Bear, however, did not go as well as planned.

Although the location we had chosen was at elevation and continually blessed us with great weather, the Big Bear Lake area provided little to no space in which to train on a flat surface. The hilly and uneven trails caused injuries to my feet and knees that I'd battle for the next six months. No matter what I did, I could only seem to last a few days before the pounding would be too much for my lower body. This led to fewer quality training days strung in a row than I'd desired. And as my spring hopes morphed into summer frustrations, it became clear that training in Big Bear had done the exact opposite of what I'd wanted it to. If anything, I devolved. When the clock ticked closer to qualifying time, I knew yet another change was needed for me to have any chance at all of making the team. So, on a sunny Saturday morning, I loaded my stuff into my car and headed back down to Burbank to live with Mom and Dad, with hopes of getting healthy and making one last run toward the US Olympic team.

OUT OF TIME

Once I returned to Burbank, the flat surface turned my training around and I felt like I was back to my old self again. My miles (and my confidence) were back up and it seemed like my original plan to qualify for the trials at the Mission Bay Marathon that January could happen.

Yet again, I was wrong.

Two weeks before Mission Bay, for no explainable reason, my back seized up while I was on a run. This was not just a cramp—it hurt like hell. It was so painful that walking became a challenge. Breathing was such a miserable experience, I tried to hold my breath for long stretches of time so the pain didn't make me pass out. After several rounds of cortisone shots and treatment, I could move around pain-free again, just not in enough time to compete at Mission Bay. So, after searching high and low for a race that would still let me qualify, I flew across the country to run in the Boston Marathon. But to make a long story short, I dropped out, putting a period on any real chance I had to qualify for the 1976 Olympic trials.

To say I was disappointed would not be accurate. It was heartbreaking. I had put an incredible amount of sacrifice and hard work into those four years and to see it all slip away so quickly was hard to wrap my head around.

Still, the one thing that remained a constant light in my life was The Streak. I was still totally in love with getting out each day, and although there were no trials on the horizon, knowing I could still get out and push myself each day increased my confidence not just about running, but about life. It affected my confidence by offering something I could accomplish each day, allowing me to be physically active, and providing something that was just for me. Those runs after Boston gave me the opportunity to be alone with my thoughts and the dirt trails, reflecting in a way that many people don't get a chance to. There I was still doing an activity I loved, an activity most other athletes saw as punishment, and no matter if I raced or not, I could still run each day—and enjoy doing it.

Little did I know my life would soon change yet again, this time not at Griffith Park or on San Vicente Boulevard, but on the 101 Freeway.

Glendale Community College Archives

Charlie Dimarco, myself and James Harvey

QUESTION: When things didn't go the way you planned, especially with a long-term goal, what did you do to move on to the next challenge? If you don't handle unexpected changes well, what could you do in the future to make these transitions easier?

BACK TO VALLEY

In the late spring of 1976, my former teammate from L.A. Valley, Mike Wagenbach, and I were in my car, driving down the 101 freeway on our way to work out, when a familiar face pulled up beside us. Driving at about fifty miles per hour was Nick Giovinazzo, one of the assistant track coaches from Valley. He stuck his head out the driver's side window, the wind ripping away at his hair, and shouted at the top of his lungs to ask what we were doing. After we both yelled back that we weren't doing anything, he told us to stop by his office in the next day or so, because he might have a job for us. We gave him a thumbs-up, he waved good-bye, and we headed off to train.

When we stopped by the campus the next day to see if he was bluffing, he offered us coaching jobs that we accepted faster than it took to run a 100m dash. Within a few days, we were signed up to teach physical education classes and work with the distance runners. Nick also told us that if we obtained graduate degrees, we could make some real money and even have the chance to make coaching a career. Although I was in great shape, the sun had set on my dreams of a running career and with age thirty right around the corner, earning a certificate seemed appropriate and not too challenging. I enrolled at California Lutheran University, took graduate courses at night, and within two years, received my master's degree in education with a concentration in physical education. That degree kick-started my teaching career for the next four decades.

And, of course, I still ran every day.

CREATING A CULTURE OF MY OWN

Even though I had already coached a team to a state championship at Glendale, the short duration of that stay, on top of the fact that I'd still been trying to get my feet wet with coaching, made me feel that this opportunity at Valley was the first time I could really take ownership of a group. I wanted to take what I had learned from my own experience as an athlete and concoct a training formula that presented an atmosphere of accountability, competitiveness, and comradery in which everyone could succeed. It didn't matter if you were a 4:40 miler or a 9:05 two-miler, I wanted everyone to walk away from the program better than they were before they arrived. It was my goal to provide them with skills they could use in every aspect of their lives—just like my coaches had done with me. Step one in that process was finding the right mixture of positive people and extraordinary talent through recruiting, which was one of the things I had come to really enjoy during my time at Glendale.

What made this recruiting season unique was that this was when women began to enter junior college athletics across California. When women first arrived on the team at L.A. Valley in the late seventies, none of them (sadly) came from schools in which they'd run high school track and field. These women had only run in gym class or on their own. My philosophy about the addition of women to our program was simple—treat them with the respect they deserved and don't be afraid to train them hard. The accountability standards were the same, the language was similar, and the time investment was identical. The men on our team graciously embraced these women as members of our team, even when the women occasionally beat them.

The final piece to our newly created culture puzzle was finding the right set of assistant coaches to fit our group. During our first year, Mike and I worked with every event on our team, sharing coaching responsibilities. I would suggest that every coach take time to do this at one point in their life, along with those in any type of management position. Observing each member of the group you are leading and experiencing, discussing, and most importantly, learning what their specific group needs makes you a better leader. It's hard to motivate a person if you don't know what the hell they are going through or how to correctly communicate with them. So, Mike and I learned about every event, and how to talk to the kids and provide effective insight. Still, as the team grew, we clearly needed some help. That help came in the form of Charlie DeMarco, who would work with our throwers and jumpers, and James Harvey, our new sprint coach.

QUESTIONS: If you are leading a group, do you understand all the roles that comprise it? How do you communicate with those members of your team who you don't work with on a daily basis?

James was born in Harlem and, after moving to California with his mother in the 1960s, he had run for Long Beach Poly High School and attended college at San Jose State University. This was at the tail-end of the *Speed-City* era, the nickname given to the school's track team at the time, which included Olympic 200m gold medalist Tommy Smith and silver medalist John Carlos. Upon meeting one another, James and I connected like drops of water. It didn't matter that we'd grown up in different environments or that he was black and I was white. Other than his tendency to speak so fast it was at times hard to understand him, he was an incredible coach, an outstanding motivator, and the most devoted person I had ever come across when it came to being a support mechanism for the kids on our team. If anyone needed anything, James was around. If you needed to work out late, he would turn the lights on in the stadium and stay until the sun came up. If he needed to sleep in the office to do an early workout, that is what he did. James was such a presence on our team with his energy and enthusiasm, many thought that he, not I, was the head coach (something I was one hundred percent okay with). With James's energy and knowledge, Charlie's expertise in field events, and my experience with competing at a high level, we created an environment that was not only the most fun I had as a coach, but one that produced individual and state champions nearly every year for a decade.

"Mark's and [James] Harvey's team at Valley were not meant for weak people. Mark knew how to say things about each guy on the team that would go right at their ego, while Harvey never wanted to be around people who were full of shit. If you were someone whose feelings could be easily hurt, those teams were not the place for you. You left those teams with mental toughness, an understanding of the importance of consistency, and a unique ability to attack challenges that never left you because of how much it was engrained in your psyche each day. Even now at the age of sixty, I still compete in masters track and field, road races, and cycling. And it was the lessons I learned from those two years with those two coaches that affected how I would go on to train, coach my own teams, and live for the rest of my life."

Steve Brumwell
Athlete, L.A. Valley College 1976–1978
6x Los Angeles Unified School District Girls' Basketball Coach of the Year (Ulysses S. Grant High School)
2x Qualifier, World Masters Track & Field Championship (5,000m)

But it wasn't teaming up with James and Charlie, or the success we had at Valley, that made my time there one to remember. That happened when a long-haired brunet with an amazing smile walked into my jogging class in 1977.

DEBI

I was taken with Debi Alberts the moment she stepped foot onto the track at Valley in the spring of 1977. She was a student in my jogging class at the time. Prior to applying to Valley, she'd read *The Complete Book of Running* by Jim Fixx and decided that she would give it a try. When she saw I was teaching the class, she recognized my name. Apparently we'd attended the same high school, Debi being three years younger. As you may have noticed, I took training and coaching very seriously and never pursued much of a romantic relationship. I ran, and now I coached, and that was pretty much it. But Debi had a natural disposition that made it easy for me to talk to her and after our last class ended, I gathered the courage to ask her out for a hamburger. She said "yes," and eighteen months later, we were married in October 1979. I've been lucky enough that she has stuck with me to this day.

Running had been the most important, if not the only thing, that mattered in my life from the time I was sixteen. And now, as I was nearing thirty, I was coaching a team of my own, I was no longer training to win a national championship or to make the Olympic team, was building deep friendships for the first time as an adult, and (most importantly) I had a partner who understood how important The Streak and running was to my life. The most important thing during that part of my life wasn't training or coaching or how important each piece was toward The Streak—it was the relationships I made and kept that would keep The Streak alive for the next thirty-five years.

PART V
PEOPLE, PLACES, AND HOW
TO JUMP OFF BUILDINGS

TIME FRAME: July 24, 1976 – December 31, 1988
TOTAL DAYS RUN CONSECUTIVELY: 7,466
TOTAL MILES RUN: 92,661
BIGGEST MILEAGE MONTH: 467
TOTAL DISTANCE COVERED: 12.46 round trips
across the Atlantic Ocean
HISTORY:
- Pac-Man is released
- John Lennon is killed
- The first IBM-Personal Computer is released
- The first cell phone call is made
- Nike releases Air Jordan 1's
- The Internet is developed

I ran every day.

THE STREAK CONTINUES
—WITH SOME HELP

Relationships are hard. Anyone who tells you otherwise either doesn't know or is lying to you. The main reason they're so challenging, at least in my opinion, is that relationships are a constant. They constantly present situations that cause you to examine your level of commitment to other individuals or groups, they test your loyalty, and if they're to remain successful, relationships require a level of sacrifice from both parties. The relationships I built and the situations that took place in my life in the mid-80s didn't just strengthen The Streak, they helped carry it through toward the next century while bringing greater meaning to my daily runs. And, whether I was coaching or selling concrete grinders, it was the people I met and gained insight and knowledge from who allowed me to get where I wanted to go.

Relationships and running are incredibly similar. Success in both requires internal strength, a dedicated support team, and most importantly—love. There are exciting times and not-so-great times. There are times where you can't wait to get out the door and get going and those when you want to stay at home and become a permanent piece of your couch. Situations may arise that you would rather not address, but to move forward, something must be done or said. In running, that could be addressing injuries, and in relationships, it could be confronting your friend or partner. Running involves pain, from sore muscles to dealing with failure. Where defeat after a competition may pull at your heart strings for days after, confining you to your room like a hermit, the same can be said when you have a fight with your best friend or you go through a bad breakup.

During the early years of The Streak when competing and winning championships were my primary goals as a runner, that competitiveness always acted as the catalyst for perseverance when times became tough. To be successful, to be one of the guys, and to compete on the elite stage— that's what drove me. But when those days concluded, it was just me, my shoes, and the road. There were no races to win and no podiums to stand on.

Because of the support I received from Debi, my running streak continued and our newly formed coaching staff at L.A. Valley had a four-year run that was as successful as any community college team in California. Jumpers, throwers, sprinters, women, and men—all exceeded the level of success we'd obtained when I was a student-athlete at Valley fifteen years prior. At that point, I was still running over one hundred miles per week, but as someone who loved to train hard *and* run tons of miles, putting in high-quality, high-intensity work while coaching was impossible.

Of course, there were times where I wished I could have been racing, but I was an old guy (in my 30s) and being grounded in my life was much more important to me than chasing a dream that wasn't going to happen and making those around me suffer. Just like my father was for my mother, I wanted to be a good husband and be present for Debi when she needed it. The same went for the team, as I didn't want to give the perception that my racing was more important than anything we were trying to accomplish as a group. Still, I really enjoyed training, discovering if I could do things in practice, and pushing myself in ways others couldn't push themselves. The thrill I received from my support system, both at home and at work, ended up being just as rewarding, if not more so, than any of the accomplishments I'd achieved in the dozen or so years of The Streak that occurred before we all met.

> QUESTION: What are the relationships that matter most to you? Why do they play a significant role in your life?

GREAT TEAMS, GREAT ACCOMPLISHMENTS, AND GREAT STRUGGLES

We had some great teams at L.A. Valley during the early part of the 1980s. We had someone either compete to win or win a state championship every year, and that success led to us continually recruiting top athletes, both male and female, from every corner of Southern California. The formula of effective communication, the incredible motivation James provided to every aspect of our program, and seemingly superior training proved to work for us time and time again. Of course, like any coach will tell you, we needed the right type of student-athlete, and luckily were able to get kids who had a willingness to be coached and a white-hot desire to get better.

> *"Other than my father, no person had a greater impact on my life than Mark. When I think about him, I don't think about his running streak. Of course, The Streak was and is a big deal, but what I think about is how much it meant to him that we all improved, along with the deep-rooted love he had for running. When you saw how much he was into it, it made you want to be more engaged and do well because you didn't want to let him down. It made the relationship you had with him stronger, because you were so aware of how well he wanted you to do. And when you saw he was running every day, although he didn't say, 'Hey, get your ass out there every morning at 6:00 a.m., because that's what I do,' you saw the type of person he was and how incredible a person and runner that made him. So, not taking any days off just became a part of who you were."*
>
> **Andy Ligeti**
> L.A. Valley College cross country & track team
> 1979–1981
> History Teacher, Jefferson
>   Community & Technical College

But like most events in life, where there are highs, there are also lows.

I had received my graduate degree, which allowed me to teach some classes at Valley while I coached, but honestly, the combination of those things didn't produce much money. Our first son, Chris, was born in 1982 (James was his godfather), then first our daughter, Brittany, two years later, and it was clear I needed to find something that paid the bills better than part-time coaching and teaching. (I should mention, I did run on the days Chris, Brittany, and my other children, Patrick and Ashley, were born. Debi was nice enough to have the kids during times that allowed me to get my run in each time.)

Debi stayed home to take care of the kids, and just like my dad had been, I was the lone breadwinner for our family. We weren't flat broke—I know there was an unthinkable number of people who struggled to find work in our country at that time—but for us, it was incredibly challenging.

To make things even more fun, after not getting a full-time coaching position at L.A. Valley in 1984, I made the difficult decision to walk away. What made it especially tough was that I had to leave coaches I had built strong relationships with—and right when the program had found its stride. I desired to coach, but more importantly, I needed a job that could support my family. Luckily, I quickly found what I was looking for—sort of. My coaching urge was filled by becoming an assistant track coach at Los Angeles Trade Technical College, which was in downtown Los Angeles. Simultaneously, with some help from my father-in-law, I did get that full-time job. But it wasn't in teaching or anything related to athletics. Frankly, it didn't matter to me what the hell I was doing, as long I as I could support my family. And a few weeks later, I was on a plane to Connecticut, on my way to learn how to sell construction accessories.

The life of a construction accessory salesman may sound lackluster at first mention, or seem as if it has nothing to do with running, but as I said, life and running have an incredible amount of similarities.

A NEW DEFINITION OF THE STREAK

The Streak took on many definitions during its evolution. It was birthed by accident, evolved into something that helped get me into college and obtain a degree, then became the thing that helped me keep my Olympic hopes alive. But after my competitive career had concluded, The Streak became about one thing and one thing only—love. I loved, and still do love, to run and train.

Love is challenging, exciting, and invigorating. But it can also be destructive, painful, and traumatic. Love makes us do things we never thought we would do, it transforms us into people we never thought we could become, and it allows us to discover who we are, what we want to do, what turns us off, and what lights us up. For me, the love of running created ankle sprains, bruises from falls on dirt trails, muscle strains, bursitis, and inflammation. But it also created raised levels of adrenaline, a runner's high when I was in a groove, confidence upon the completion of a two-hour run, and an internal strength that provided me with the thought that if I could push through pain and focus when I was uncomfortable, there was nothing I could not accomplish.

I loved the sensation of stepping outside in the morning when you could hear a pin drop. When the only things in front of you are steps you haven't taken yet. When a question is presented to you that asks, "What can you do today?" or "How hard can you push yourself?" or "For how long can you concentrate?" Each of these things simply made me feel better. No matter what I had going on with my life, from the struggles of trying to find and keep work, to eventually being on the road 150 days per year selling construction accessories—I could still go out and go for my run. When I went on my run, I could be like a horse with blinders that allowed me to just focus on the road, my effort, and the step that was happening in that moment.

Now, you are probably asking, "Wait ... you were on the road 150 days per year?" Yes, I was. "And you still ran every day?" Of course, I did. My new job was not centered around a desk. I after a week of training, I became their Western region sales executive, a position that put me on the road to discuss and sell their products. That Western region turned out to be half of the United States. My meetings took me from the snow of Denver to the rain of Seattle, from blazing heat in Phoenix to cutting winds in Salt Lake City. When I had trips to San Francisco, I would rise at 4:00 a.m., go on my run around 4:30 a.m., pick up my rental car at 6:00 a.m., drive up to the Bay Area and arrive around 1:00 p.m., have all my meetings, and drive back, getting home around 1:00 a.m. Then I would get up in the morning and meet my team for practice at six the next morning.

This part of my life, if you couldn't already tell, was stressful.

But just because something is stressful doesn't mean you half-ass it. It means you create ways to forge through it.

Now look, there are lots of people, probably some of you reading this right now, who have faced or are facing shit that is a lot harder than what I went through. I was lucky enough to have a job, an amazingly supportive wife, and healthy children. There were plenty of people, especially in the 1980s, going through some *really* tough times. I say this because I don't want you to feel sorry for what I went through; rather, I want to paint a picture of the choice I had each morning. I could have stayed in bed during those days on the road. But plain and simple: I loved running, the people around me knew that, and their ceaseless support encouraged me to keep it going.

My support team also understood my daily runs were just for me. It was something I could do for at least thirty minutes after being on the road all day, and it always made me feel better, because I had accomplished something just for me. Now, call that selfish if you want. It is. But I am a firm believer that each of us should have a portion of the day in which we are selfish. At that time, we should do something we love that allows us to feel great. It could be yoga, reading, playing an instrument, going on a walk, or a hundred different things. But doing something you want to do, that improves you mentally or physically, and that is only for you—those are the times where we will vastly improve our emotional and mental health.

QUESTION: Is there something you do each day—
just for you—that you feel helps improve your mental
and physical health? If not, what can you do with
your schedule to create thirty minutes a day to do so?

BE THERE AT 4:30

During those days on the road, I visited cities with some extreme weather conditions. I learned to enjoy traveling, but not because of the flights and cheap motels. Rather, it was all the unique ways I was able to see different parts of America by getting up early, going for my run, and absorbing an unfamiliar city—especially during a time of day when most people would never experience it. While many would spend the day standing in lines to look at monuments and dealing with crowds to get perfect views of scenery, I was able to see it all either while the sun was coming up or right before. Those were special times just for myself and they allowed me to do and see things in unique ways I will always remember.

Some of these visits, however, were more unique than others.

If you have ever been to Phoenix, Arizona, in the summer, you know how exceedingly hot it can get. The average high during the month of July is around 104 degrees. This leads businesses, especially ones that required working outside, to have peculiar work hours. On one specific instance, I got in to my room in Phoenix in the early evening and made a call to the foreman of a company I was trying to sell concrete accessories to. "Well, it's pretty hot this time of the year, so we get to work pretty early," he said in a scratchy voice. "That's not a problem," I told him. "Alright," he said. "We'll see you in a few hours. We start at 4:30 a.m." I admit, I was a bit shocked. "Wait, what time?" I asked. "4:30 a.m," he repeated. "It's gonna be over a hundred degrees by nine, so we try to wrap up before noon."

I told him I would be there, but as I hung up the phone, my thoughts went immediately to my run. There wasn't a question in my mind I was going to get the next day's run in, it was more so a matter of when. It would either have to be in the heat, after being out with the construction guys all morning, or before that—really, *really* early. Well, I made a questionably smart decision to wake up at 2:30 a.m. and headed out the door to get my run in at 3:00 a.m. It was a comfortable 70 degrees and I got to see downtown Phoenix during a time when it was practically deserted. And although I was a bit tired, the feeling of accomplishment from knowing I got my run in and saw the city in a unique way was worth it.

> QUESTION: When you travel, do you squeeze in a workout or anything else that gives you time to yourself? If you don't, what can you do the next time you travel to provide some time to yourself?

DON'T BE A VICTIM

I have discussed at length in this book how important it is to put your head down and grind things out. The challenges you face each day will do their best to take you down and it up to you to either get up or stay down. To succeed in tough situations, you will need resolve, grit, and perseverance or odds are you won't achieve what you want.

When you're in a relationship with someone, whether it's a teammate, your coach, your best friend, or your partner, and things are tough and you feel like nothing is working, or like the world is going to end tomorrow and nothing can go right, or like you suck at life and will never be any good at anything—that's when you begin living life as a victim. Instead, you need to regularly communicate with yourself in a positive manner. That's something my parents began to instill in me when I was younger. Walking around playing the martyr will not help you get anywhere. Self-victimization and complaining do not have any real value. All they do is lengthen the distance between you and your goal. Realizing you have control of your situation and then acting on it is more powerful and contains more real value than any amount of bitching or complaining ever will. The direction of your life is not set in stone; you are the one who must choose whether you will be the victim or the hero of your own life.

The reason I bring all of this up while discussing relationships is because when you make the decision to become the victim, you make everyone around you miserable. No one wants to associate themselves with someone who constantly complains about how tough their life is. If relationships are about connections and sharing, then of course it's okay to discuss where your head is at and the concerns you have about situations moving forward. However, when something becomes a chronic issue (like excuses, for example), then you have something that will poison not just your life, but the bonds that connect you to those you care about.

When you stop being a victim and come to the realization that things are happening for a reason and the world is not out to get you, your life will become easier. The people who care about you do so because they believe in you; they believe in you when you win, fail, or tie in any experience. That's what real relationships are. They are bonded together by experiences. Great relationships, just like the body when you run each day, can handle the rigors of stress. Bad ones, like going for a long run with little training, can be hard to handle and will eventually break apart.

There were plenty of times during The Streak where I really felt like shit. But I understood this was part of the price of running every day. So, I always did what I needed to do so my mood or state didn't affect those around me. Debi took care of the kids while I was gone for work half of the year. My kids didn't have Dad around as much as they probably needed. And my team had a coach who wasn't around all the time. The last thing I wanted to do was be the guy who walked through the door after being gone for a few days and complained about how things were going.

That's why I made sure I was around during birthdays, anniversaries, and other big days when I was needed.

That's why I got an ultrasound machine at home so I could treat myself before I went on my runs.

And it's also why, when in the summer of 1986, after I ran in Canyon Country, California, and broke my foot while attempting to jump over what I thought was a rattlesnake, I still continued to keep The Streak alive.

QUESTION: Have there been situations, whether in life or in training, in which you have acted like the victim? What were the reactions of people around you when you did so?

THE BOOT

In the early 1980s, our family moved from Los Angeles to Canyon Country, which was located just twenty-five minutes from Trade Tech, and although it was a commute, it wasn't too bad. Canyon Country was a beautiful place to train, with dirt trails that accompanied rolling hills in nearly every direction you turned. In the morning, especially during sunrise, due to the area's lack of large trees that would usually create shade for them to rest in, you would occasionally see a snake make its way across a trail. I always did my best to stay away from them, but one late summer morning, something went wrong.

I was about three miles from our house, when I thought I saw a snake directly underneath my right foot. As soon as I noticed it, I tried to get my foot out of the way and upon doing so, wasn't sure if I landed in a hole or right on the snake. As soon as my foot hit the trail, I heard (and felt) a loud snap. The pain shot up my leg and sent me to the ground. I rolled around in the dirt for a bit, just screaming at the top of my lungs. It hurt like hell. It was as if a bolt of lightning had risen from the earth and was delivered directly up my leg. Once I calmed down a bit, I noticed my foot had become unrecognizable; it was swollen to at least three times its normal size and was completely black and blue. Knowing I still had to get home, I decided to tie my shoe as tight as humanly possible and tried to hobble back home. When I hopped in the door on one foot and told Debi what had happened, she immediately threw me in the car and took me to the hospital. I wasn't sure if The Streak was over, but things sure didn't look good.

After some X-rays in the emergency room, the doctor determined my fifth metatarsal was broken, but not as badly as it could have been. It wasn't a complete break, which would have led to surgery that day, and an automatic end to The Streak at around twenty years. This may sound a bit crazy (well, this whole story may sound crazy), but there was one lucky thing that happened through all of this.

Because of how swollen the foot was, it turned out the doctor couldn't put a cast on it. He just told me to wrap it up as best as I could and come back when the swelling went down—so *then* he could put a cast on it. Well, as you might have guessed, I didn't go back to get casted up. Once I finished my run the next morning—which was, to say the least, an excruciating experience—I went to see my podiatrist, John Pagliano.

John was more responsible for The Streak lasting forty-five years than any one person was. I always referred to him as the "doctor to the stars," because if they were famous and had foot problems, they were automatically sent to see John. He worked on Magic Johnson's feet during his plantar-fascia issues, and he helped nearly every athlete on the Los Angeles Rams, along anyone else you could think of in Los Angeles.

When the two of us had first met in the 1970s, I was at Fullerton and he was road racing (which he did frequently, finishing the Boston Marathon on multiple occasions). After a local 5K, we were introduced and once we got the small talk out of the way, he told me if I ever had anything he needed to look at, to give him and call and he would be happy to help. From that moment on, his assistance, his friendship, and his treatments lasted for close to half a century.

What made the relationship between John and me so strong was that we had shared philosophies about how to deal with my running. Not once during any of our appointments did he ever tell me I couldn't continue to run. **He was committed to finding solutions, to discovering alternatives, and to making things work—a mentality that was for me, a perfect fit.** Visits to John's office were always bit of a trek; he was located near Long Beach, the epicenter of traffic hell in Los Angeles, but they were always beneficial. Every time I was looking for a solution, I knew John would have the answer. When I broke my foot, I had been his patient for over a decade and he had seen lots of aches and pains related to my running, but nothing as bad as this.

After I plopped myself on his examination table, he took off the bandage and upon seeing the extreme discoloration and massive swelling, just like the doctors who had examined the foot the previous evening, he concluded that a cast would be impossible. He also concluded that I needed something that *acted* like a cast. Something that was big enough to stabilize my foot and ankle, but at a minimum, allowed me to jog around. Once we'd chatted about some potential solutions, I mentioned I had some very thick, very heavy construction boots back at the house. I asked John if that could be a potential problem-solver, and he didn't say no. He did tell me, however, that a typical break of this type would have put me in a six- to eight-week cast. However, because of my running and needing to be on my feet for work, my recovery, if I was lucky, would be twelve weeks or more. I really didn't have a problem with that at all. If I could still get up each day and move around, I would be okay.

So, for the next three months, I would wake up each morning and wrap my foot, put my construction boot over that foot, lace the boot up as tight as I could handle, and head out the door for my run. (I admit, the first three weeks of this venture were not pain free.) When I wasn't running, I did my very best to stay off the foot, including days when my team had cross country meets and I would use crutches to get around. It took quite some time for the swelling to go down and even longer to get my natural running stride back. But after two months, things were finally getting back to normal and after twelve weeks, the construction boot was finally retired, and I returned to my Nikes.

My experience with the boot went down as a humorous legend during the remainder of The Streak. Many people who heard of it thought I made it up, while my wife and children have made jokes about it for years, mainly because of how ridiculous the whole thing was. **Even more than a lesson in not being a victim, the boot taught me the importance of forming relationships with people who have the same mentality as you.** Remember, rather than viewing negative situations in a light that can crush your long-term goals, look at them as teachable moments; it makes them much easier to overcome.

Successful people surround themselves with successful people, and those who aren't looking to do much affiliate themselves with those who are looking to do much of the same. If you think about those who have achieved remarkable things, from Gandhi to King, Carver to Edison, you'll find people in their universe who understand the importance of their success and are driven to do important things, as well. Lazy people are not vital to others' achievements. Instead, people who don't do shit tend to hold back those who might otherwise succeed.

Over the course of The Streak, I tried to surround myself with people who wanted to do exceptional things. They were those who were looking to innovate in training, treatment, and rehabilitation. The phrase "this can't happen" or the word "no" was not a part of their vocabulary. John was one of those people, along with many others who would come along during The Streak's later years.

No matter the problem, there is almost always a solution. And whether you are running, working, going to school, or whatever it is that matters to you, having a support team that is driven to help you, wants you to be successful, and understands what your goals are is just like building a home with a solid foundation. Those who build their homes in the mud are likely to sink. But those who build a foundation of strength, rigidity, and durability will last the tests of time.

> QUESTION: Do you have a support team?
> If so, who are they and what do they do to
> help you? If not, what can you do to build one?

MORE NEW JOBS

After a few years on the road, I'd gotten my fill of airplanes and motels. The kids were getting older and I wanted to be around more, so after another conversation with my father-in-law, I left the construction company and began work at Build-It Engineering Company, which my father-in-law owned and my brother-in-law ran. I continued to coach at Trade Tech and, because I didn't have to be out of town every few days, I was able to spend more time around my family. It was an improvement for everyone. My one hundred-miles-per-week training days were long gone; however, I was still running about seventy-five a week and was in good shape for someone in their mid-thirties with a few kids.

Build-It was a wonderful place to work. Through our dealings in the engineering world, I ended up crossing paths with a Japanese company that specialized in producing and selling a piece of safety equipment they called a Dissenter. In Japan, during the 1980s, because of the population density in large cities, it was required that all skyscrapers have multiple escape routes in case of fires or other emergencies.

Dissenters acted as another escape route. Each apparatus came with several hundred feet of one-third-inch steel cable and a harness. Once the harness attached to your waste, in an emergency, you would jump out of the nearest window and descend securely to the surface beneath you at the speed of three feet per second. When I discovered they were in search of a salesman and paid more than what I was making at Build-It, I decided to make another career change. Although it involved a bit more travel, I could still coach (now at Canyon Country Community College in Santa Clarita, California, the town we called home for a few years in the mid-1980s). Having been a salesman for a few years at that point, I felt like it was something in which I could succeed.

And I got to jump off some buildings.

JUMP

Since the Dissenter was the main product I was promoting, I had to give lots of live demonstrations across the country, doing my best to prove to Americans that this thing could work. I presented in front of members of US Congress, risk management companies, police and fire departments as a new way to implement safety across their cities. Many of these demos were done at fire department training stations, where the most I had to jump was about four stories. I figured if the device failed, it wasn't going to be a long fall and, being around people who knew how to save lives, I would be okay.

But then I had a demonstration in Indianapolis.

When I got the call that I would need to travel to Indianapolis to do a Dissenter demonstration, I was told that this time I wouldn't be doing my presentation at a training station, but a building. I was curious how high the building would be, but really didn't think much of it. The address for the presentation was somewhere in downtown, which was filled with large high-rises, and after my morning run, I suited up and headed to the twenty-two-story building where I would give my pitch.

After giving my presentation in the conference room, I pointed out the window and explained to everyone that I was going to show them how it worked. Once I strapped on the harness, I looked straight down and was suddenly scared shitless. Twenty-two stories is a big increase from the four stories I was used to. But I knew showing fear in my face or body language would have flushed the deal right down the toilet. I took a deep breath, stuck one foot out the window, and after getting the other one out, created a ninety-degree angle with my body and spoke to everyone about what I was about to do, while they just glared at me through the windows. As I looked directly into their eyes, they seemed more concerned than I did that I might plummet to the sidewalk and crack open like an egg. As the wind picked up and my grip tightened, I began my walk down the building, taking one step at a time, just like I had done in dozens of track and cross country races for years before this. I made it to the bottom with a round of applause. (Although I think they cheered more for the fact that I didn't die than for the Dissenter, because they didn't purchase any from us afterward.)

LANCASTER

My junior year of high school, we'd had a meet scheduled against Antelope Valley High School, located about sixty miles north of Burbank. I had never been through Lancaster before, and had never met anyone who visited. Reason being, as I found out, it was quite the hike to get there. During a time in which there were no main highways that reached the Antelope Valley, the only way to get to the area was via Sierra Highway, a road built in 1910 that weaved its way in and out of the San Gabriel Mountains, eventually reaching the desert on the other side. As our bus zigged and zagged between brown mountains peppered with dry, brown-and-light-green bushes, you could feel the air turn cooler, hear the wind gust louder, and watch the sky grow darker. Once we crested the top of the mountains, the Antelope Valley appeared with a vastness that could only be described as breathtaking. Joshua trees, something I'd never seen before, lined the two-lane highway, and dust danced through the air, landing and creating thick layers as tumbleweeds wheeled across the road like hundred-meter sprinters. We didn't see many homes throughout the drive, and until we reached the center of town, where the wind gusted and the clouds shifted from light gray to dark black, we didn't even see a stoplight.

Once our team got off the bus, with no large buildings or hills to hold back the thunderous wind gusts, no one could get over how cold it was. It was so frigid, Kallem even gave us permission to run in sweats—something he'd never done before, nor would he ever again. I raced the mile and two-mile in that meet, and after ending the race with two second place finishes, nothing—I mean nothing—made me happier than getting on the bus and going back home. Lancaster, though beautiful, with its beige and reddish yellow sands that painted the ground, wasn't a place I was eager to get back to once we returned to Burbank.

Still, in 1989, twenty-one years since my junior year of high school, with a family that had grown to six after we added Patrick in 1986 and Ashley in 1988, we relocated to the place our family still calls home this day—Lancaster, CA.

FINALLY

The commute between Burbank and Lancaster was a bit over an hour. Five days a week, my routine was to get up around 4:00 a.m., leave the house as close to 5:00 a.m. as possible, drive down to Griffith Park to get my run in, shower at my parents' house, and get to Build-It, which I still used as an office when I worked for Matsumoto, by 8:00 a.m. Those days reminded me of when I'd commuted back and forth to Fullerton during my red-shirt year. My days were long, sleep was minimal, and work was abundant. I was never one who handled commuting well. Lots of people I met over the years would tell me about how much they loved spending time in the car and listening to the radio a few hours a day. That was not me. So, although my family was in a good place and work was going well, my work situation was not one I was particularly crazy about continuing for much longer.

One thing that made Lancaster appealing to me was its community college, Antelope Valley College, known around town as AVC. Located on the opposite side of town from our home on the east side, AVC at the time had an enrollment of about 8,000 and was the only college or university in the Antelope Valley. Throughout my coaching and competing experiences, I had seen their track and cross country teams compete and although they rarely had outstanding teams, they always had individuals with some talent. I decided to give the college a call and see if there was a way I could work with the team. It was a roll of the dice, but just like the countless cold calls I made for work, I knew if I could get the right person on the phone, I could seal the deal.

Brent Carder was a legend in the Antelope Valley. Having been the Head Football Coach at AVC for over forty years, Brent was now the head of the athletic department and one of the most respected members of the community. He was also one of the winningest coaches in California Community College Football history. Knowing my best play was to talk to the man in charge, I gave him a call one afternoon from my office in Burbank. He picked up the phone right away, and when I told him who I was, he mentioned he had my name on a note that was sitting on his desk, along with my phone number. Somehow, word had gotten to him that I'd moved into the area and he should give me a ring. After a few minutes of chatting, he said he would love to have me involved with the program and that I should stop by to meet with him and the head track coach, Dick Curtis.

I began working with the distance runners almost immediately and, after only a few months, I was told that there would be a position opening after someone retired. He suggested I apply for the coaching job. I did and a few months later, for the first time, I was a full-time head track and cross country coach, which included a full-time teaching position. After twenty years of part-time jobs, twenty years of hotels and red-eye flights, twenty years of running in unusual places at 5:00 a.m. all over the country, I could finally get up in the morning, drive a few miles, and go to work.

Luck and timing had lots to do with me getting that job. But more than that, it was the support and understanding from Debi, my kids, and my support team of those in the coaching community that allowed me to become a full-time coach and teacher. To say this job was a relief doesn't fully describe it. It felt as big as winning any championship. And as lucky as I was to have been in the right place at the right time, I would never have arrived in that place if it weren't for the strength of my relationships, and my refusal to become a victim when things got difficult. The journey wasn't easy and it continually tested my faith, but nothing great ever is easy.

Meanwhile, The Streak continued to thrive and would for more than 8,500 days until it finally ended.

And as incredible as it was to land that full-time coaching and teaching job at AVC, creating a winning team—that was another story.

PART VI
MARAUDERS

TIME FRAME: January 1, 1989 – July 23, 2000
TOTAL DAYS RUN CONSECUTIVELY: 11,688
TOTAL CAREER MILES RUN: 123,658
BIGGEST MILEAGE MONTH: 305 (August, 1991)
TOTAL CAREER DISTANCE COVERED: 7.58
Round-Trips from Los Angeles, CA, to Sydney, Australia
HISTORY:
- Hubble Space Telescope launched
- Cold War ends
- Nelson Mandela released from prison
- Gulf War begins
- Amazon.com founded
- The Chicago Bulls Threepeat (twice)
- Bill Clinton elected President
- L.A. Riots take place
- O.J. Simpson Case takes place
- Atlanta hosts the 1996 Olympic Games

I ran every day.

THE DESERT

Deserts are unique places to live. They're desolate places, filled with nothing but brown weeds blanketing dry dirt where very little can truly thrive. The desert's a place where if you visit only a few times a year (or less), you really don't recognize change. The tumbleweeds still blow, the earth is still dehydrated, and the air always seems thin. But if you live there, as I learned, you come to understand that change is frequent. That along with its vast nothingness, there is beauty in the ever-changing wind and landscape of the desert. That although things may seem dead all around, you are always surrounded with hope and opportunity.

When we moved to Lancaster in the late 80s, there was a housing boom beginning, families from Los Angeles were migrating north, and the vast desert was morphing from a sea of Joshua trees to an ocean of tract homes. Although I had changed jobs multiple times in the 80s, I wasn't a huge fan of change unless it was absolutely necessary. I liked a routine. I enjoyed getting up at the same time each morning, going into an office, and turning in at the same time each night. My parents were creatures of habit and routine and that consistent day-to-day repetition was part of why I'd begun The Streak in the first place. Growing up I learned that you simply got up in the morning and went and did your thing. Sick, hurt, sad, excited, whatever. But change, adaptation, adjustments, were things I did because I had to, not because I was crazy about them.

I define change as life happening in real time. It happens every second of the day. Just now, as you read this, your body is changing. Your life is changing. The world is changing. Although I was a fan of routine, I also learned that routines change. As I continued to evolve as a coach and read countless books on training and leadership, I learned that all successful people *must* evolve. They are folks who accept change, adapt to it, and discover ways to succeed. **Learn to become available and determined; it will help you deal with changes in your career, and your life.**

QUESTION: Are you going through changes in your life right now? How are you dealing with them?

GETTING STARTED

Antelope Valley College sat on the west side of town and was smaller than the other campuses where I had worked previously. Having coached around the greater Los Angeles area where student populations touched nearly 20,000, AVC had just under 7,000 students. It was an older campus, but the large oak trees that paved the walkways, the Joshua trees that surrounded the campus, and the snow-capped Tehachapi Mountains in the distance presented a serenity that was very different than the freeways and loud streets that surrounded L.A. Valley, Glendale, or Trade Tech. And because of the lack of housing around the school, the campus was a great launching place for our distance runners.

Our track was a jet black, rubberized surface that could only be described as disappointing. Large potholes graced most of its lanes and the roaring wind made it a tough place to train. We did, however, have some fantastic grassy areas on the practice football field and baseball field that we used to train throughout the year. Having some softer surfaces made recovery easier after hard days, but our meet days were *exceptionally* long, because we couldn't host any meets and had to travel every weekend we had a competition.

The goals for the program were simple: get high school kids in the area interested so we could eventually compete for conference team championships and get to the state meet. These were the same goals as every place I'd coached before and although I was now in a place with a much smaller population and a program without much history, there seemed no reason to me that my goals for success should change.

My first team at AVC was so small, we could easily fit both the men's and women's teams into two Dodge Caravans. With fewer than ten people on each team, just like I had when I began coaching at Glendale nearly twenty years before, to create the team I was looking for, I needed to recruit. The problem was, nobody there had any clue who I was or my history as a coach or athlete. Many coaches wouldn't return my calls. AVC was not popular with high school coaches in the Antelope Valley. AVC was not a sign you were continuing with your education, but that you had failed in getting accepted into a four-year school.

It was viewed not as a place to get a quality, inexpensive education—but as a place where you *had* to go because you had no other choice. And with no scholarships available to community college athletes in California, that made it even harder for us to get great athletes to attend AVC.

This of course was all bullshit. A person could save money by living at home, take the same classes, and receive much more attention than they would if they went to a university with 30,000 other students. Then, with some arduous work and luck, maybe they'd even be able to receive a scholarship to a four-year school. That seemed like a pretty good deal to me.

What I needed was someone who could come in and prove to athletes around the area that, one, I could coach and, two, an investment in community college was a true investment in their future. It was a nearly identical situation to the one at Glendale before Bobby Thomas committed.

This time Jean Harvey, a lanky brunet with a choppy stride and incredible talent, would answer that call.

Jean was the third child from a family of eight, many of whom would end up running for me after she graduated. Her parents were both involved in the local running club, and as a senior at Paraclete High School (the same school all four of my kids would attend), Jean would finish in the top fifteen at the California Small Schools State Cross Country Championship. I was lucky enough to get a sit-down with her and her parents to talk about AVC, even when it seemed like a done deal that she would attend UCLA. At the end of the meeting, I knew I had one last chance before I left to make a pitch. Having been in this situation seemingly hundreds of times during my time as a salesman, I went for broke. "Jean, UCLA is a great school and I am sure they can find you a place on their team. But your parents are going to foot the bill for your schooling and continue to put your brothers and sisters through private school, which won't be cheap, either. My personal and professional opinion is to give your parents a break. If you come to AVC and save some money by staying home and paying very little for your tuition, you can train with us and become a great runner. Not a good runner, but a great runner. And we will get you a full scholarship to anywhere you want."

A few days later, Jean called the house (we didn't have cell phones yet) and told me she was not going to UCLA, she was coming to AVC. Now that she'd held up her end of the bargain, it was my turn to try to hold up mine.

BEING AVAILABLE

I don't believe you can deal with change unless you are available. People who are stubborn and unwilling to adapt to the ever-changing word around them are the opposite of available. They expect everything to work for them and believe the world would be a better place if everyone were just like them. When things go south, they pass their failures on to others to avoid the blame. **Those who are available are open to criticism, willing to change how they train, and ready to do the things necessary to become what they want to be.** As I discussed previously, once you reach a new level in a job or at school, you must be willing to recommit yourself to more strenuous work. None of that happens, however, without being available to make the change.

Being available allows you to be more consistently present and in the moment. If you're unavailable, you're just living your life on a treadmill, unable to see or take advantage of things that come your way. While others may have a clouded vision of who they want to be, available people are tuned in to who they are and realize that anything can remove them from their path. When you talk to them, they are truly present. When they look in the mirror, they know who they are in that moment. They are available and awake enough to notice exactly what is happening emotionally and physically with themselves and others. And, most importantly, they are not against using new strategies, so they can be successful.

Jean Harvey, on the podium after finishing second in the 10K at the 1991 TAC/USA Junior National Championships.

When I first met Jean, I understood how availability was part of change, but she epitomized how being available could help a person ascend mountains that may have once seemed impossible to climb. She made me understand the importance of that skill. The decision to attend AVC was not an easy one for her to make, but her availability would allow her to achieve the things she wanted to—and then some.

QUESTION: Would you consider yourself someone who is available? Are you able to adapt to change easily if it means it will make it easier for you to achieve your goals? If not, what things are holding you back?

SIGNS OF HOPE

Just because recruiting was tough didn't mean for one second that my determination, resolve, and will to do great things at AVC was weak. In fact, it had never been stronger. I fully understood that the road would be long and the path sometimes as isolating as the far-reaching parts of the desert we were living in, but I was not frustrated. Rather, I was filled with excitement about the opportunity that lay ahead. I had the chance to change kids' lives through a program I knew could be successful.

During this time, my morning runs were filled with thoughts of what needed to be done and how my team and I could make something special happen. The thrill of once again building something from nothing, or not much, didn't just get me fired up to come to practice or go to meets, but to get up each morning and continue The Streak. It wasn't that it was in jeopardy as the 90s began; hell—it lasted another two decades. But I discovered that when you get up in the morning to do something, even if it is something you enjoy, having other parts of your life going well makes the things you like to do even more invigorating.

I was still fit at that time for a guy who had just turned forty, and for Jean, someone who had never run more than thirty miles a week in her entire life, it made a difference when I ran with her and the other members of the team. That was a big piece of how we began to make the march toward becoming the program I wanted to be. If we didn't start our runs from campus, we would run in the hills located five miles from campus, with a meeting point in the parking lot on the corner of 30th Street West and Avenue P. Those trails and hills acted just like Griffith Park had for our teams at Glendale and Valley in the 70s and 80s. That was where we could challenge one another, create unique variations of runs each week, and measure where we were and how far we had come (or needed to go) in our training. We met at 6:00 a.m. every day except Sunday and with the daytime temperatures easily reaching over 100 degrees in the summer, early runs would allow us to beat the heat and go out for an easier workout in the evening when things began to cool down.

I didn't immediately make Jean run 100 miles a week; however, we did double her mileage to around sixty-five to seventy-five miles-per-week and increase her intensity during her freshman year. She seemed to respond well and stayed injury free as the cross country season went along, and at the 1990 Southern California Cross Country Championships at Mount SAC, she received the last qualifying spot to the state meet. Going into that meet, we talked a lot. We spoke frequently about the course, how to execute our plan, and what thoughts Jean may have at certain parts of the race. Lots of coaches enjoy long meetings with their teams leading up to big meets with the hopes of motivating them to victory. They'll have their team jog the course a day or two before a big meet, then talk again. Big speeches are nice, but preparation is better. Based on what I'd learned from my time coaching and being coached, I wanted to be as involved in the planning process as possible, not just via typical discussion and visualization, but since we had run together so much already, I wanted to practice with her on the course during that pre-race run. There we could discuss tactics, along with how she should visualize each critical moment in the race.

We broke the three-mile race into a multi-chunk battle that would have multiple changes and differing goals. Jean understood the effort needed, the execution that had to take place, and, most importantly, the plan we had created going into race. If she could just stick to the process and not worry about what may or may not happen, she would be pleased with her finish and happy with her time.

Not every competition goes the way you plan. You can plan, talk, stress, re-plan, and go over the potential scenarios in your head over and over, but you won't know what is going to happen until you go out and execute. That is the difference between dreaming of great things and going out and getting it done. It's important to be available in these situations so we don't miss what is happening around us, what our internal dialogue is like, and how to best react when the time is right.

Those who are great and who are "available," no matter what the challenge, will get the job done.

And on that Saturday at Mount SAC, Jean did just that.

Jean executed the plan we set out to perfection from the first step to the last. She finished seventh overall in an incredibly difficult field (again, she had been a thirty-mile-per-week runner in high school only four-and-a-half months before that). After that finish, I thought we may have something here. Her excitement afterward wasn't only a result of all her hard work, but an indicator that she was ready to attempt a larger volume of runs and try to achieve something remarkable. That race also strengthened our relationship, because it proved to her I could keep up my end of the bargain. Jean knew if she trained hard, she would be have the chance to not have to pay for her education once she finished AVC.

THE NEXT STEP

Since we had recruited some great athletes, our team was beginning to pick up steam. We were still in the infancy phases of building something special, but it was clear our athletes and staff were moving in the right direction. As Jean's star was on the rise, we had two other athletes of exceptional work ethic and talent (a nice combination) who were ready to take the state by storm.

The next piece that kept us moving in the right direction was our throwers. They were coached by Steve Stokes, who although he'd never coached throwers before, was one of the hardest workers I had ever come across. He wasn't afraid to talk to other coaches about training, he was a non-stop figure at clinics, and he would spend hours on end watching film. It also helped that he was incredibly enthusiastic and created an environment that turned good kids into great athletes. The first of those athletes was Angie Arington.

Angie had come to us via the college's basketball team and was a natural in the discus. She was not afraid of intense work and within a few weeks of working with Stokes, she had become one of the state's best. On the men's side, we added Larry Johnson, who had transferred from Moorpark College. Being 25, Larry was a bit older than most guys on the team and along with having a body that was born to throw the hammer, he was a man on a mission. He was as determined and as focused to become the state champion as any person I had ever come across. And by the time the season started, it was clear he would be the man to beat at the end of year.

At the 1991 State Track Championships, in less than ideal conditions that included pouring rain and howling winds, both Angie and Larry ended the year the way they wanted: with state titles. Jean would fail to win both the 3,000m or 5,000m at the state meet that year. But although Jean didn't have the type of meet that met her standards, she had run fast enough to qualify for the United States

Track and Field Junior National Championships in the 10,000m, which would take place two weeks later.

To say she made up for her poor performance at the state meet would be an understatement.

Jean finished in second place, qualified for the USA's Pan-American Team, and in doing so, broke the national junior college record for the 10,000m. After she returned from that meet, one thing was clear—she was ready to win a state title of her own. She did just that a few months later at the state cross country championship. Shortly after, Jean would accept a full scholarship to the University of Arizona and go on to become a NCAA All-American in cross country for the Wildcats.

I had kept up my end of the bargain.

"Coach Covert really helped me believe in myself. When I had made the decision not to go to UCLA, it wasn't easy, because everyone knew I had been planning on going for months. But once Covert told me that if I ran at AVC I could get a full scholarship to college, I knew staying home and training with him was the best decision I could make. It turned out to be the best choice I made as a young adult. I had goals I wanted to achieve, and he showed me that dreaming big and expecting more of myself was okay—I just needed to put in the work. And during that point in my life, I was able to do well in school and still excel at running, which again, was something I don't think I would have been able to accomplish if it wasn't for him during the two short years he coached me. Coach Covert never told me to stop trying to do big things, train less, or run slower. He believed in what I could do. That made me believe in myself even more."

Jean Harvey
1991 Cross Country California Community
  College State Champion
Former National Junior College record holder, 10,000m
Cross Country All-American, University of Arizona

DETERMINATION

I was determined to build a competitive program at Antelope Valley College. Throughout my life, and especially during The Streak, being driven and determined were traits on which I prided myself. I understood how being determined was vital to positive change. I had to deal with injury but keep training, deal with issues at work but keep running, deal with stuff at home but keep going. While I was incredibly driven to do great things at the college, keep The Streak going, and remain a great husband and father, I didn't have to look far to find someone who was outperforming me in her level of dedication; for me, this person redefined determination.

A few years after our daughter Ashley was born, Debi mentioned she was thinking about going back to college to become an elementary school teacher. Not only was she tired of working long (and late) hours at the hospital as a receptionist in admissions, but she also wanted to act as an example to our children. She wanted to show them the importance of an education, that if she could get her degree in her early forties, while continuing to work and deal with the five of us, then they could do it too. Debi's drive was remarkable. Her routine consisted of staying up all night studying, going to class after taking the kids to school, then heading into work and getting home close to midnight. Several times, in a high-energy house with four kids under twelve, she had to do her studying inside one of our cars parked in the garage to find a quiet place to study.

Debi was a straight-A student at AVC and Chapman College, and received her teaching degree in just three years. From then on, if there was ever any point in which I bitched about how hard things were for me, while I stood outside in the sun with a stopwatch teaching people how to run, I would think of Debi and what she was going through and had gone through for us. She served as a constant motivation to all of us. Her level of determination and grit toward achieving her dreams was something I had never seen before. What I had done up to that point with my running seemed easy. What Debi did was hard—but she was determined.

> QUESTION: Is there someone whose determination has inspired you? What did they do?

THE NEXT PIECE

As our team grew and began traveling in busses rather than minivans, it was clear we needed more help. Coach Knox (who, after spending nearly twenty years in the Army, had attended AVC in the '80s and, at the age of forty, won the conference championship in the 100m) was an outstanding coach for our jumps and sprints, but with the growing size of our team, he needed someone to give him a hand with the sprinting events.

Turned out I had worked with someone before who I thought could help.

There are times in your life when something happens that is simply meant to. Call it destiny, fate, or whatever you want to name it. I never believed in that much until one day, it happened to me. One morning, I picked up the phone and dialed James Harvey's number, thinking that he would be the perfect fit for our new sprints job. After punching in his digits, the phone didn't even ring, he automatically picked up. Turns out, he was calling me at the same time to see if he could come to AVC. James was going through some frustrations at L.A. Valley and although coaching with us would mean he'd have to commute an hour back-and-forth a few days a week, he was more than happy to join us. I was thrilled.

What made our reunion even more exciting was the fact he was going to bring some athletes along with him who would really help our team. He was still a big name in the Los Angeles area and could get in to speak with every high school coach he called. During a time when community colleges couldn't recruit anywhere in the state (that has all changed now), his ability to bring kids to the desert and potentially do great things helped transform our program from good to great in just a few months. We began to produce individual and team conference champions in nearly every event, and we began a new streak at AVC—we'd send at least one athlete to the State Championship in cross country and track every year I was head coach.

It was an exciting time for us at the college.

Unsurprisingly, we dealt with situations that forced us to adapt to change. Hell, I would be full of shit if I didn't admit everything eventually changes. It's up to us to figure out a way to deal with it. Either we freak out when things get tough, or we go and make things happen. We must do what we need to do to adjust. **As important as it is to be available and open to change, without determination and grit, you will never do the things you set out to do or become the person you want to become. (Remember, positive change, like nearly everything in life, is not just one thing; it requires learning a set of skills and combining them into one powerful tool.)** Once you have the skills toward making a positive change at your disposal, you can deal with almost any unplanned modification to your life plans.

I learned that all too well in the spring of 1996.

WHERE IS GEORGE DANIELS?

My family was always busy. Dance practice, dance recitals, soccer practice, soccer tournaments, swim practice, club swim meets, club basketball practice, city basketball games, cross country practice, cross country meets, track practice, track meets, Catholic Education classes—these were all typical parts of our lives once school got out each day. Debi and I would switch off most nights between taking and picking up the kids from their different events, and I although I was busy coaching and teaching, I was still able to make it to (and sometimes coach) nearly all their games and major events.

In the spring of 1996, Debi and the kids came and picked me up after the state track meet, which took place at Cerritos College, on their way to a soccer tournament that one of my kids was playing in. "How did it go?" Debi asked. I really didn't know where to start; the tale of that year's state championship didn't begin with the story of our first race, or even our best race—but rather what had happened before we left campus that morning.

I remember it being an absolute perfect spring morning as the kids loaded up the vans to head to the track season's last meet. As good as we were all feeling about the upcoming championship, that feeling turned to anger when we did a headcount. "Where the hell is Daniels?" James asked everyone repeatedly early that Saturday morning as the sun had just started to crest the mountains in Lancaster.

"Coach, I told you, I don't where the fuck he is man," was what he heard time and time again. George Daniels was at the core of the best team we had going to the state meet that year. He anchored our 4x100m relay team that was ranked top three in the state, he was ranked second in the 400m going into the state championship, and he anchored our 4x400m relay team that we believed had a chance to win.

The guys on the team ran to pay phones and called George's apartment to see if he was there, but no one answered. We were now running fifteen minutes late. Then thirty minutes.

Still no George Daniels.

After we had been waiting at the vans for almost an hour, our anger had transformed into concern. No one could get ahold of George via phone and after guys on the team pounded on his door for twenty minutes with no response, both James and I thought something bad had happened. No one shows up over an hour late, especially for the state meet, right? The issue we were running into, however, was time. We had kids competing in just a few hours and we couldn't throw the meet in the toilet because of one athlete. When we looked to our team members, the expressions on their faces said clearly what needed to happen: "We know George isn't here, but we gotta go."

So, after nearly an hour of waiting and still no George, we took off.

You may be thinking, "Wait, you only had three members of your relay teams on the bus, what the hell did you do when you got to the meet?" Like I said, when change and adversity hit you in the face, if you are determined to make it work and not freak out, you can still make something remarkable happen. When you work in collegiate athletics, you are paid to be the calm force in front of the kids when times get tough. The last thing you want to do as a leader is make everyone around you a wreck because you can't keep your shit together. Leaders increase the level of enthusiasm, while decreasing the level of stress of those around them. In this case, as concerned as we were for George, James and I didn't want to ruin our kids' great year because we were pissed off at the situation. The best thing we could do was stay calm and try to figure out something when we arrived at the meet.

When we got to Cerritos more than an hour later than scheduled, there was still enough time for the relay team to check in and get warmed up. James and I talked on the track as the guys jogged around, when out of thin air, our solution appeared.

Joey Moore, a tall, bleached-blonde-haired, athletic kid with a chiseled frame, was our decathlete who hadn't qualified for the meet, but was there to watch his girlfriend, Kristine Bostick compete. (Kristine was our school record holder in the 400m hurdles at the time and would later compete at University of California at Irvine.)

"Holy shit, what about Moore?" I asked James. We didn't have cell phones at this time, so when Joey got there, he had no idea what was going on or what he was getting himself into. James sprinted up the stands and asked Joey if he still had his uniform. Turned out he did. James said, "Great! Go warm up. You are anchoring the 4x1." Joey didn't even ask why or what was going on, but grabbed his stuff out of his bag and like someone who had just won the lottery, sprinted over to the guys on the relay team, and began to get ready. He adapted to change and accepted the challenge as if it were natural to him.

I have discussed at great length the importance of coaches (or leaders) encouraging others to believe in themselves. Even if the odds are against you and the situation is grim, if the person leading those into the field of battle has their troops convinced they can achieve something remarkable, that's often all a group needs to make something miraculous happen. That is what James was at both Valley and AVC. He was the kind of leader who could look you square in the face and against all odds and all inner belief you were going to fail, he'd make you believe something special was going to happen.

James had the guys ready to go and after the first three legs, we handed the baton off to Joey with our guys in second place. The kids at the meet who knew what was going on were going absolutely nuts. The guys had a remarkably clean handoff, and Joey ran his ass off, but without the pure 100m speed to match the state's top sprinters, our team ended up in seventh. The relay guys were disappointed at the result, but the coaching staff and other members of the team couldn't have been prouder of the effort that they'd put in considering all the shit they'd been through. We did everything we could not to allow them to victimize themselves, but rather use their seventh-place finish as a tool to kick ass in the 4x400m.

The team had a good meet that day and going into the 4x400m relay, we still felt that even without George, we could be in the top three. James had trained everyone on the team to run the 400 meters. It didn't matter if you were a power sprinter or a long sprint specialist, everyone had done the preparation to allow them to race one lap around the track. Joey had done his job in the short relay, and when we needed to solve our long relay dilemma, we turned to our top 100m man, Kenny Hopson. Kenny had attended Monroe High School in the San Fernando Valley and would later compete for the Yellowjackets at Georgia Tech. He was known for his immense talent, his even more impressive work ethic, and for never backing down from a fight. This would be his third event of the day, and knowing what it meant to our team, he warmed up with the long relay like someone who had the confidence of a 4x400m veteran.

Once James had given his last words to the group and they made their way to the track, he walked over to me, and his body language made it clear these guys were ready to go. James was a big Spider-Man fan. When we went to meets, rather than wearing our team shirts, he would wear a Spider-Man hat and shirt. I never minded it. It was his way of being himself. And as we stood there in the setting sun, the long shadow of the stadium beginning to cover the track, me in my sweat-soaked Nike hat and James in his Spider-Man apparel, with as long a day as we had just been through, both of us hoped for a victory.

And that is exactly what we witnessed that evening.

Our leadoff leg, Varick Dabney, got us out right with the leaders. The baton then went to Mike Price for leg two, who surged down the backstretch, keeping us right in the mix as he handed off to Mo Bakcus. After getting the stick in second place, Mo made the exchange to Kenny in third place with one lap to go in the state championship.

Kenny was everything but shy when he got the stick from Mo. He ran right around the turn, chasing down the leaders, and as they came through the backstretch, deep into the shadow of the stadium, he made his way onto the outside of the lead pack. This created a line of the top four teams, straight across the track, with 250 meters left. With 200 meters remaining, Kenny made his move to the inside, trailing the leader by only a step as the crowd continued to grow louder. With 100 meters to go, Kenny fought like a madman, but didn't have the strength to outrun the state's top anchors. After Kenny nearly collapsed across the finish line, AVC's 4x400 meter relay team, minus the state's top 400-meter man, finished fourth overall at the state championship.

I've been involved in track and field since the 1960s. I have watched lots of big meets and have been lucky enough to be a part of several memorable moments. But that day at Cerritos College was hands down the most incredible and moving moment I've ever witnessed in the sport of running. The heart and will those kids showed that day was something that still to this day, blows me away.

There is a saying that goes, "If your will is strong, your feet will become light." Well if that is true, the wills of Kenny Hopson and Joey Moore allowed our team's feet to run on clouds.

When we found Kenny after the relay, he was laid out on the warm-up area and could barely move. He had never done anything like that before and his effort had really taken a toll on him. When James and I picked him up to shake his hand, he told me something I always will remember. I said to him, "Kenny, that was simply remarkable, the effort that you put in. I gotta ask, how did you do it?" He replied simply, "Harvey told me I could do it."

"If there was anything I learned from being around [James] Harvey and Covert, it was in order to accomplish anything, you have to be mentally tough. During our 1999 track season, we had a slew of injuries to the guys on our relay team that could have ended our season early. But our coaches believed in us when we didn't believe in ourselves. Harvey used to tell us to 'get the punk out of your heart.' And that wasn't just something he told us about running—it was about being a better and stronger man. He had you believing you were this strong man who could do anything when you were on that track. We would go on to win the conference championship in the relay that year with a team that probably shouldn't have won, but we believed we could and our coaches knew we could. It was the type of environment that made you proud to be involved each day."

Craig Carson
Former Track & Field Athlete,
Antelope Valley College, 1997–1999
Member of the 1999 Foothill Conference
Championship 4x400m Relay Team

After I told that story to Debi and the kids (with the kids laughing and smiling throughout the entire tale), we drove across town to the soccer tournament, still not knowing where George was, where he had been, or what we were going to do if we ever ended up speaking to him again. I spoke to the paper that night after Chris's soccer tournament was over, and told them about our little episode, and two days later, our town newspaper's sports page headline read, "Where is George Daniels?"

I still had no idea where he was. Neither did James.

Then early Monday morning, seventy-two hours after missing the van, George showed up at our office.

Luckily, nothing tragic had happened to George that Friday morning. He was simply late and expected us to wait for him. He said when the guys had come to his house and pounded on his door, he never heard it as he was still asleep. He was pissed we hadn't waited, but James and I were over it. I was relieved to know he was still alive (we had discussed calling the police if we didn't see him that Monday), but I also knew we had made the right decision in leaving when we did. Other people on our team were meant to shine on a day that went down as one of the great days in our program's history. Sure, we didn't win a state championship, but if you learn anything from this book, you should know that though you may not win the championship, you can still put in a championship effort. And at the end of the day, win or lose, that is all that matters.

MOM & DAD

The other challenge that came along in the 90s was dealing with my parents' failing health. They had moved up to Lancaster shortly after I had become the head coach at the college, settling in a three-bedroom house on the other side of town, only four miles from where we lived. It was great having them so close, not just because we could spend more time together, but because they could spend more time around the kids—which both my parents and the kids loved. Both Mom and Dad where never ones you would consider in poor health, so when I got a call one afternoon from Mom that I needed to get to the local hospital, it was a frightening surprise.

Early that morning, Dad had driven himself to his doctor with pains shooting down his back and in his shoulder. The doctor told him he had been playing too hard with his grandkids and he should go home and get off his feet. Well, as the day went along and the pain got worse, my brother (who was living with my parents) had to drive Dad back over to the doctor. He saw his primary care physician who, after examining him, determined he'd had a heart attack. The doctor immediately placed a nitroglycerin tablet under his tongue, put him in an ambulance, and sent him to intensive care.

The doctors were unsure if he was going to make it through the night.

In the big picture of The Streak, it's when there were conflicts or traumatic events (not just team or work stuff) happening in my life that going for my run each day deepened in meaning. Although most of my runs during times like this were short (mostly less than forty minutes), they always gave me a chance to take a deep breath. When I was out running, I wasn't sitting in a hospital waiting for a doctor to come and give an update, dealing with stress at work, or anything else that took me out of the emotional and mental state I needed to be in to function optimally.

When things were bad with Dad, it felt as if I were in some type of haze. I wasn't available at all. When I was at work, I wasn't at work. When I was at the track, I wasn't at the track. Running presented a situation in which I only focused on the run itself. It was as if the dirt from the trails and the yellow-and-orange glow from the morning street lights were an anxiety relieving medication. When I returned home, I was always in a better place. Not just a better place for me, but for my mom, Debi, and my kids.

> QUESTION: When you have had a traumatic event happen that changed your life, how did you deal with it? If it was not in a healthy way, what could you have done to address that change better?

Dad ended up improving and after two long weeks at the hospital, with only forty percent of his heart functioning, he was told he could head home. Being the tough guy he was, giving in was not something he had in mind. The determination he showed to have a normal life was incredible. But it wasn't only his will to live that fueled his body to adapt. Less than a year after Dad's heart attack, Mom was diagnosed with breast cancer. Shortly after that, the doctors noticed her eyesight was going and she was pronounced legally blind. Then, as if things weren't bad enough, Dad, with his heart miraculously improving and his spirit still strong, took another health blow when he was diagnosed with esophageal cancer right after Mom lost her sight.

It was a lot to handle. For everyone.

But somehow, as Mom got worse and struggled both emotionally and physically, my father remained stoic. He was strong in his faith, and even stronger in his love for Mom. They had known each other nearly their entire lives and were the true definition of life partners. They weren't just spouses—they were best friends. And as Dad continued to fight and be the primary caregiver for Mom, even when his body deteriorated as the tumor in his throat prevented him from eating, my mother again became sick. This time it was lung cancer. She was gone four months after being diagnosed. They had been married fifty-three years.

After Mom's passing, my morning runs seemed to take a little longer and Dad seemed to fight a little less. He passed four months later.

James's father passed a few months after mine and with the turn of the century around the corner, I was turning fifty, my kids were getting older, and change was happening almost everywhere I looked. When change takes place in your life, you try to do what you can to stay afloat. You might cry, run, meditate, spend more time with your family, or whatever you need to do to get you through that moment. Availability and determination can help a person deal with change in a healthy way. Like I said at the start of this chapter, change takes place with every new second of each day. With each second you grow older, and hopefully wiser, and are presented with an opportunity. An opportunity to show the strength of your will, commitment to your values, and the ability to achieve incredible things.

That is why, through all my life's developments, I still ran each day. I ran to achieve something over which I had total control and that would fill me with a sense of accomplishment.

And as the century ended, The Streak still had 4,952 days remaining.

PART VII
FAREWELL, OLD FRIEND

TIME FRAME: July 24, 2000 – July 23, 2013
TOTAL DAYS RUN CONSECUTIVELY: 16,436
TOTAL CAREER MILES RUN: 159,651 / Streak
Miles: 149,652
BIGGEST MILEAGE MONTH: 252 (July 2003)
TOTAL CAREER DISTANCE COVERED: 66.8% of a
trip from Earth to the moon
HISTORY:
- Terrorists attack the World Trade Center, triggering
  two wars in the Middle East
- Wikipedia founded
- Facebook formed
- Hurricane Katrina hits the Gulf Coast
- Barack Obama elected as President
  of the United States
- Michael Jackson dies
- The world population reaches seven billion

I didn't run every day.

LUCKY

By the time we hit the turn of the century, I had created a comfortable daily routine. I would wake up around 4:00 a.m. and, because I was teaching online courses at the time, would begin my morning by answering emails and getting some work done for about an hour. On Monday and Wednesday mornings, I would head out the door to get my run in around 5:00 a.m. My workout would include some type of interval training on the streets of Lancaster, which were only lit by streetlights and headlights of cars as they began their early morning commutes. From there, I'd head to practice that began at six o'clock. On Tuesdays and Thursdays, I would still get up at 4:00 a.m. to do class prep, and get my run in with the team during their practice. I could still run with the slower guys on the team then and would usually break off halfway to see where everyone was and check on how they were feeling.

Practice would usually wrap up a shade past seven o'clock, where I would then go and shower on campus, grab a bite to eat, and head off to teach an eight o'clock health class. After a day mostly filled with classes and meetings, I would go to 3:00 p.m. track practice and be back to the house by 5:00 p.m. If my kids didn't have something going on that night, I would stay home and head to bed around 9:00 p.m. (but was usually asleep on the couch by 8:30). Then I'd do the same thing over again. This routine was not punishment or filled with negative thoughts about having to get up each morning to run. Instead, it was flush with a visceral feeling of excitement.

The most successful people I met during my time as an athlete and coach each seemed to have a routine that made them want to get the day started. I considered myself lucky to be one of those people. I was and still am someone who does not like surprises. Having my day planned out and knowing what I needed to accomplish each day reduced my anxiety and made me feel comfortable. When something did come up that was unexpected, I was able to make adjustments to my day, because I still knew what I had to get done that day before I turned in. A routine is just another piece of preparation. And as I mentioned at the start of this book when discussing toughness, when you are prepared, you can do great things.

QUESTION: Nearly all successful people have a morning or evening routine that allows them to either get their day started in the right direction or presents an opportunity to reflect on their day. Do you have a routine, either in the morning or evening, that prepares you to start the day on the right track?

At this stage in my life, The Streak was a big deal. It was the longest running streak in America at the time, and I was lucky enough to have been featured on *The Today Show,* and in *Los Angeles Times*, *The New York Times*, *Runner's World,* and countless other print and TV news outlets for being so consistent (and for seeming kind of crazy). Nearly everyone would ask me in interviews whether The Streak was hard. Was it something I felt like I had to drag myself out of bed each day to do? Or was it truly something I did with no hesitation? My answer was always the same, that ninety percent of time, The Streak was easy. It was easy because it was something I was excited to do. As I have mentioned several times, getting out the door each day and doing something where I could push and challenge myself each day was fun. It was fun to find out if I could run one loop faster than I had a week before, or how much I could concentrate when I felt uncomfortable, and, although I was not as quick as I had been in my competition days, whether I could still create the feeling of my body moving fast.

My job at the college played a significant role in allowing me to continue to keep running each day, because training with the kids on the team, I felt, was vital to our team's success. I'd run with them, see how they looked, and discover if they were running a certain time on a loop, all while getting my daily run in. I was incredibly fortunate. And I *understood* how fortunate I was. I didn't have to go into a job each day that I hated, dealing with traffic and/or a boss who was a prick. Getting up and doing something I loved doing was my job. How lucky are you when you get to do that?

> QUESTION: Is there a healthy activity you do each day? If not, what would you like to do and what adjustments can you make in your current routine to make it something you do each day, if only for a few minutes?

When it came to the team, after over a decade of trying to make AVC's a program that gave kids the best opportunity to become successful, I felt we had accomplished what we set out to do. Coach Knox, Coach Harvey, Coach Stokes, Coach Syler (who would replace Stokes in the later part of the 1990s), and I had turned a program that didn't have much of anything into one we felt was competitive. We had several teams at the state cross country championships place in the top ten and we sent athletes to the state track meet every year. Because we lacked the numbers other teams had in the Los Angeles area, we could never be a team that competed for state team championships, but other teams knew we'd compete hard and be right in the thick of things when it mattered. Much of that success came from convincing the kids that the regular season was not as important as the championship. While many programs focused on each meet as a "big deal," we focused on meets at the end of the year. And because most of the time we were coaching athletes with average talent, they blossomed when we told them they could win championships if they trained hard all season. Remember, we only worked with student-athletes for two years and then they were gone. Our job was not just to teach them to run well, but to excel in their classes and move on to a four-year school. While many of our kids went on to Division I, II, and NAIA schools on scholarships, nearly everyone was able to gain a sense of accomplishment and skills that would help them well past their years on our team.

That was something I, and our coaching staff, was extremely proud of.

"There are two things I learned from those days with Covert that I still use today. First, he taught me the importance of having a plan. A plan for everything. I was a fly-by-the-seat-of-your-pants kinda guy in high school and never had much of a plan for what the next day would look like. I would just get up and go. But he showed me that to be successful, you must have a plan. It's something I tell every athlete I work with now. That's why they keep journals and we never do something that is not already scheduled. Secondly, Covert showed me how important it was to have courage. Before we started working together, I loved to sit in the back of races and try to out-kick people in the last 200m. He made me believe I was good enough to get right to the front with the most competitive guys in the field and take it to them. In 2000, at our conference cross country championships, I was incredibly sick with a sore throat and fever, but it never crossed my mind that I shouldn't run. Covert asked if I could run and because I didn't want to let him or the guys down, I said, 'yes.' That was a special day for me because not only did I win, but to do so with the illness I had proved how courageous and tough I could be when I needed to. I had to be taken to the hospital that night because I was so sick, but still made it to practice the next morning for our long run. That is how much you wanted to show how brave you were."

Daniel Cobian
Foothill Conference Cross Country Athlete of the Year, 2000
Foothill Conference Cross Country Champion, 2000
Strength and Conditioning Coach, Chicago White Sox
Baseball Organization

After nearly a decade of making the commute up to Lancaster from Los Angeles, James decided the 2002 season would be his last. It wasn't an easy decision for him and it certainly wasn't easy for me to come to grips with, knowing this was probably the last time that we would work together. He re-joined L.A. Valley's program shortly after returning home, but didn't coach for long after health problems arose that plagued him for the rest of his life. He suffered a stroke in 2008 and two years later, during a routine trip to the dentist, was informed he had cancer of the tongue. The last thing James and I did together was special. In 2010, we were both inducted into the L.A. Valley College Athletics Hall of Fame, where he was nice enough to ask me to introduce him.

James Harvey, better known as Uncle James to my children, passed away shortly after his diagnosis; he was only fifty-three years old. It was a hard moment not just for our family, but for the countless numbers of people he inspired through his continuous encouragement, tough love, and honesty. We all still miss him to this day.

SURGERY

The desert always seems filled with distant memories. It's that place where life altering hikes can happen, where one can take long drives and glance out the window to see nothing but tumbleweeds for miles on end, and if you are someone who has spent thousands of miles on those trails like I have, it's a place where you see memories in the form of trash. In the dunes people will place couches they no longer sit on, rusted bikes their kids no longer ride, or bags filled with garbage that somehow seem at home under the shade of a Joshua tree. Spending as much time on desert trails as my team and I did, you learned to always keep your eyes peeled. You look for stray dogs, people you may know out on their own run, or for a left-over memory you may have to hurdle. I had gotten used to hopping over stuff during my runs for over a decade in Lancaster, especially behind the college where stray logs from old building projects were randomly scattered behind the athletic fields. But one early morning in 2003, less than two minutes into my run, while attempting to jump over a log I had jumped more than one hundred times per year for the past decade, I misplaced my steps, falling directly on my left kneecap.

The journey that followed created another memory for the desert.

The fall itself was not that big of a thing. Falling is something that, after running every day for nearly forty years, I knew was part of the deal. Every once in a while you're gonna slip on something or trip over something you just didn't notice. When I got up and dusted the dirt from the front of my shirt and the sand off my knees, everything seemed normal. There were no cuts or bruises, and after spitting some dirt out that had gotten into my mouth, I was on my way. After getting back to campus, I noticed my left knee cap was a bit sore, but it was nothing I didn't expect. A few days later, however, it was hurting so much that each time I would roll over in bed, I couldn't do so without moaning. I went to an orthopedist, and after an

MRI, they determined the fall had caused the meniscus in my left knee to tear, which would require surgery.

I understood what surgery would do to my knee and more importantly, that there was a chance The Streak could end because of it. That understanding was something with which I found peace. If it needed to end because of this, then it was meant to end at this time. However, just rolling over and having someone tell me The Streak could end, especially on terms I didn't agree to, was not something I planned on. The only way I was going to allow The Streak to end was if there was no other option. If there was a pathway for me to keep it alive, I wanted to explore it.

Before my trip to the doctor, I had done some research about the trauma knees experience after surgery. What I discovered was that it wasn't necessarily my meniscus that would need time to heal after the operation. More so, my knee itself would be traumatized after being sliced open, having steal implements shoved in it, and then sewn back up. To me, there seemed like no reason I couldn't run after the surgery was completed.

To most people (okay, almost everyone), running just a few hours after an operation on your knee seems crazy. But again, I was at peace with the situation, calm in the moment, and saw a path that would allow me to continue The Streak *and* get the surgery, all while maintaining my knee's health. The doctor, understanding my personality and my situation with the streak, scheduled the surgery to take place as soon as possible. A week later, I got up at 3:30 a.m., got my run in an hour later, took a quick shower back at the house, and headed over to the hospital for my 9:00 a.m. procedure.

The operation was quick and successful, and allowed me to head home around 2:00 p.m. Other than being a bit sore where the cut in my knee was, I felt fine. Getting up the next morning to head out for my run, however—that was a challenge. The less-than-potent pain medication, combined with a strong compression sock that went from the very top of my hip down to my ankle, was incredibly uncomfortable. Debi and Chris drove me out to a space of open desert a few miles from the house as the sun was coming up on that freezing December morning in Lancaster. When I got out of the car wearing a big coat and gloves, the sock was still on and although I knew I would get my run in, *how* I was going to achieve it seemed unclear until I put some weight on my leg. Once I stood up tall and put some pressure on it, I realized I could jog. It was going to be with a hobble, and not the prettiest thing, but it was good enough to work. That morning I ran a mile with my cast on, less than twenty-four hours after surgery, in a little over ten minutes.

I always knew The Streak would eventually end. I also knew it would end on *my* terms. The words of a doctor, although valuable, were never going to be the end of something I had overseen since I was eighteen years old. You can call that idea stubborn, even dumb, that's fine. But The Streak was up to *me*. The number of miles I ran each day was *my* decision. Getting up each morning at a specific time was a choice *I* made. Training through illnesses was what I selected to do—no one else chose that for me.

And as the years of The Streak continued, the events that threatened it became more difficult to overcome. And although I knew I'd always have the final say in whether I was going for my run on any given morning, I began to ask myself—when is the right time to walk away? Am I at that point?

WALKING AWAY

Walking away from something I had done every day since the sixties was not, as you could imagine, an easy task to undertake. The challenge I had in front of me was unique in comparison to those I'd been up against in races I'd competed in, training sessions that took hours to complete, or personal tests that examined the strength of my character. Every one one us, whether the results are big or small, goes through something we must relinquish at least once during our lives. It could be removing toxic people from our lives, quitting smoking, or leaving a job that, even if it pays well, is a nightmare. Each person has his or her own reason for walking away. But within those reasons, I have found there are three specific things that should be examined before you make the decision to walk away or continue to try to grind it out.

I think you can gather that I was always trying to find a way to keep grinding along and toughing it out. But sometimes it's better for you and (maybe more importantly) the people around you, not to simply give up, but to walk away with the knowledge and understanding that you did what you could to keep going, you fought with heart, and you didn't quit, but made the best choice for you.

> QUESTION: When have you had to walk away from something you enjoyed doing? Was that decision easy or difficult—and why?

The first thing that needs to be considered when choosing to walk away from something is asking yourself if the fire is still there. Do you still have the fire inside that burned so bright and so hot your focus was never far from your goal? Or has it flamed out? If you want to achieve something remarkable, how the hell do you expect to accomplish the first step, let alone the race, if you don't have a burning passion for the things that will make you great? You must be totally head-over-heels in love with the process if you want to carry out your intentions. The second that you fall out of love with the process, it's time to examine whether it's worth continuing. I'm not suggesting you walk away from shit when it gets hard or flush your goals down the toilet when you get pissed and feel like you hate the process after a few bouts of failure. What I am saying is, the second you think the fire and passion is out, then look in the mirror and be honest whether you want to continue the journey.

It took me over forty years to have that conversation with myself. And it wasn't that the flame was gone; rather, it was the fuel that kept it burning for all those years, my ability to push hard and challenge myself, was running on empty.

FLAT FEET

Before my parents took me home from the hospital a few days after I was born, they had my feet footprinted and placed on the memento version of my birth certificate. What made these footprints different than most was that they looked like ovals with toes. In fact they were so flat, it looked as if someone at the hospital had made a mistake. The nurses told my parents they had never seen a pair of feet as flat as mine. The flatness of my feet always caused some type of trouble for me, even when I was a little kid. It was a constant battle to find shoes that fit my feet correctly. As I got older, I was always ordering orthotics for my shoes, and an ice bucket was never far away after a run.

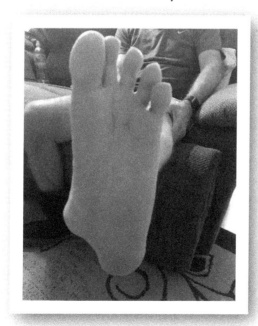

By the winter of 2009, finding ways to treat my feet had become as routine as brushing one's teeth. The pain in both feet had become unbearable; it was excruciating to the point where I could barely sleep and standing up for an extended period to give lectures in class was agonizing. I could tolerate the pain when I ran, simply because I was moving all the time and could control the surface I was placing my feet upon for an hour or so each day. After a few months of consistent pain, I noticed there was a large protrusion near the ankle of my right foot. The usual treatments of ice and anti-inflammatories did nothing, and when my foot no longer pointed straight, but veered off to the right, beginning to make the shape of a lower case "r," I knew something serious was up. It was time to see the orthopedist.

John, who you may remember from earlier chapters of this book as my lifelong podiatrist and a wizard, had passed away suddenly right before my feet started to become a major problem. I had found a new doctor, his partner Dr. Aslmand, and after less than an hour of examination, he determined I was experiencing what he called, "total midfoot collapse." In the simplest terms, the joints within my feet were beginning to degenerate. The tendons that were attached to the bones no longer had any tension, which created a situation where my foot was collapsing inside itself. The doctor didn't say I couldn't run, just that it was going to be painful unless I could find a solution via orthotics or different shoes.

Over a period of time, my foot stopped functioning.

I could wiggle my toes, but from the ankle south, that was the only movement I could make with my right foot.

This lead to my runs becoming *even slower* than what they had already been and treks where I was not lifting but *dragging* my dead foot off the ground with each step, hoping not to fall.

FALLING

I loved to train. Whether training to get fitter, or to run faster, or to see what I could do to challenge myself, nothing provided me with more exhilaration. But between the meniscus injury and then the issues with my feet, the excitement that always accompanied training began to fade away. It wasn't that I no longer loved the process; rather, it was impossible to push at a rate that made myself tougher or that gave me the satisfaction of accomplishment I'd experienced for over forty years (which, let's admit, is a long time for anything to still be exciting).

Noteworthy events happen in one's life, I believe, not just to provide opportunities to succeed, but to provide chances for reflection. This fusion of reflection, realization, and raw emotions appears when you must consider walking away from something you care deeply about. And once you get to that point, the results, although painful, become clearly obvious.

Upon reflection, I knew The Streak would have to end sooner rather than later. It wasn't because of one injury, but due to a set of circumstances that could potentially affect my quality of life for years to come.

The next step when deciding whether to walk away or stay in the fight is, when you reflect on the negative

times, do they outweigh the good (over a significant amount of time)? Training, competing, and life in general will frequently present times of failure and frustration. This is not difficult to understand. Shit, there are going to be periods of your life, whether it is a few days, or a few weeks, where thing just suck. If you aren't willing to deal with the negative stuff, you shouldn't be doing whatever it is you are doing. If you step back and examine the situation and you can't recall positive experiences while the impact of those negative times has reduced your ability to enjoy yourself, it may be time to stop. Even if what you are doing is hard, it should still be fun. Personally, when the days were the toughest, that's when I had the most fun, because I could *really* challenge myself and discover what I could do. I think lots of people forget that training and attempting to improve should be fun.

I have heard lots of coaches (especially youth coaches) say that sports shouldn't be fun, that they only exist to teach kids how failure feels so they hate losing and naturally, this will make them tougher. Some feel if kids can't deal with loss in competition or the classroom, then they'll be failures in life. I understand sports are about learning lessons (that's what this book is largely about), but I don't think you have to be miserable each time your go to practice (or at work, or in a relationship) in order to learn something. You don't need to hate just to learn more effectively. The work shouldn't make you angry or upset or hate something—it should be fun!

Jesus, if you can't have *some* joy in your work, what are you doing it for?

> QUESTION: In your current journey, whether it's academics, athletics, business, or life, have there been more good times over the past year, or more negative ones? (Be honest with yourself on this question. When people experience a string of frustrations, it's easy to say everything sucks, but that's not true. Not everything is awful. Don't be delusional.) If you're going through some rough shit, what's making it so bad?

As running became more of a physical challenge for me (at times it was close to impossible), the fun times started to dissipate. In fact, my runs went from fun to just plain painful.

A few days before Christmas in 2011, I was on my run about three miles from our house on a particularly cold day. I could see my breath as I ran. With my feet feeling better than they had been, I decided to push a bit and see what I could do.

I felt pretty good.

Then, out of nowhere, my still-dragging-behind-me right foot caught a lip of concrete, sending me diving face first into the street. It wasn't a slight tumble. When my face hit the ground, it was as if someone had come up behind me and pushed as hard as they could. I felt like I had broken my eye socket. After screaming for a few seconds, I got myself together, wiped the asphalt, dirt, and blood from my face, spit out some grit that made its way into my mouth, and jogged back to the house.

When I arrived back home and limped into the living room, Debi asked if I was okay. For one of the few times since we'd been married, I answered, "No." I went to the doctor the next day, sporting a black eye that was so swollen I could barely see out of it. The doctor determined my eye socket wasn't broken, but I still felt a sharp pain in my face each time I took a step for the next month. My runs were then delegated to short loops in three locations, each flat as a pancake with no bumps, lips, or grooves in the ground, and on well-lit paths to make sure there were no surprises.

It wasn't fun.

THE LAST STRAW

After about a year of hobbling around, The Streak had become a chore more than anything else. I was no longer gaining fitness, I was falling *at least* once a month because of the poor shape my feet were in, and for the first time since 1968, I was thinking about a day off. Debi and I had talked about getting The Streak to forty-five years and then calling it done. I wrestled with that thought for a while; I wanted to make sure walking away was something I could control and felt at peace with. Truthfully, I wasn't there yet.

The last step toward deciding to walk away is when you have begun to dwell on the past and lose focus on the present.

Everyone dreams about the past. There is nothing wrong with shooting the shit with your friends and talking about past experiences and stories that are fun to laugh about and exciting to re-live. But when the past becomes all you want to think and talk about, then you have a problem. No one wants to be like Al Bundy, constantly talking about his four touchdowns in one game, or Uncle Rico from *Napoleon Dynamite,* searching for a time machine so he could play quarterback for his high school team back in '82. We all know a person like that, and I would hope that's not who you want to become. Those who were once successful and are now struggling to regain their past glory have two options as they travel through life: 1. They can show courage by keep their eyes on the target; or 2. They can constantly look back, fully convinced that what lies ahead can't possibly be better than what they've already seen. Those whose minds are not focused on the present fail to reach their destinations. But those who have eyes on the present get to where they want to be.

I wasn't the kind of person who was always dreaming of past results or reading my journal of workouts I used to do with Tabori. That wasn't an effective use of my time, and I knew it. What I *did* think about were the times I used to be able to really focus and push up a hill, or concentrate for an hour into the driving wind, feeling as if I could conquer the world. I missed those times. I still enjoyed running, but I missed *training.* When my feelings of frustration became as bounteous as Joshua trees on the trails of Lancaster, it was clear it was time to take a day off.

Then my kidneys agreed with me.

In the spring of 2012, I came down with a case of severe kidney stones. The first of two bouts included pain I wouldn't wish on anyone. I experienced dry heaving and the type of agony I'd only associate with childbirth. I went back and forth to the doctor for a week and nothing they gave me or did fixed a damn thing. My routine for seven days consisted of getting up, running for twenty minutes, then returning the doctor's office. After ruling out any other solution, the doctor performed a twenty-minute operation and I immediately felt better.

But a few months later, the stones returned.

With a vengeance.

Along with dry heaving and a fever that was worse than ever, the pain was so incredible, it was nearly impossible for me to stand. Debi and my oldest daughter, Brittany, convinced me to go to the hospital. I was admitted instantly. I told the doctor I'd still try to run the next morning and they were going to have to deal with it. For the first time in my coaching career, I was missing a track meet due to illness and not only was I hurting, I was pissed. Pissed I was in the hospital, pissed I had to miss a meet, pissed The Streak could potentially end—and not on my terms.

My son Patrick, a history major at California State, Fullerton, at the time, traveled up to Lancaster when Debi told him I was in the hospital. When he asked how he could help, I mentioned that the doctor had written a note that said if I was feeling up to it, once a day, I could "shuffle" for up to thirty minutes. Knowing I couldn't go outside and run because of the IV bag in my arm, Patrick came up with a great plan. Turns out the hospital was only a few months old and had some floors that were still completely empty. Patrick convinced the nurses on my floor to allow us to go downstairs for my run. Their only concern was the IV, which Patrick said he would hold for me as he ran by my side.

So, on a fall afternoon in 2012, Patrick and I kept my then forty-four-year-old running streak alive. Traveling through the empty halls of the hospital, I made sure to get in at least a mile by running a total of fifteen minutes. It wasn't very fast, but The Streak continued, and I was still in control of its future. And after five long days in the hospital, I was on my way home with no more kidney stones and two very clear thoughts in my head: The Streak would end at forty-five years and, maybe more importantly, I needed to find another way to train.

> QUESTION: When you deal with repetitive failure, do you reflect on past successes, or do you try to keep your eyes ahead on the goal at hand?

MAKE A NEW FRIEND

Our family has always been big fans of the Tour de France. After my summer morning runs, most of the kids would be awake, and we would huddle around the television screen watching the last thirty kilometers through the Pyrenes or French Alps, not only cheering for our favorite teams, but admiring the sheer toughness and bravery those guys showed day-in and day-out for two weeks. I've always thought the Tour was one of the most brutal and punishing events one could go through. Riding for four to five hours a day at thirty-miles-per-hour was simply incredible—whether a person was on drugs or not. Getting on a bike myself was something that, other than teaching the kids how to ride bikes of their own, I had never considered; the very thought of it scared the hell out of me. It wasn't that I feared being *on* the bike—that was not a problem. What frightened me was the thought of *riding* in the gusting winds of Lancaster, losing my balance, and falling on my ass (potentially ending The Streak). But it wasn't until I took an honest view of my fitness during those last months of The Streak when I thought to look my fear of riding straight in the face.

My son-in-law Alexis had a bicycle he never used. When I told him I was thinking about cycling as a new way to train, he invited me over. I threw the bike in the back of my SUV and drove up to the aqueduct that overlooked the valley. That moment was the start of a relationship I never saw coming. Just a few minutes into my ride, the feeling of challenging myself returned. I was able to push myself once again. And perhaps more important than anything, cycling was something in which I could still improve. (I was humbled after my first large group ride with a local club, where I ended up finishing dead last, finally showing up to the stopping point behind young kids, and men who were ten years older than me.) I continued to run, of course, but on most days, I would run for a half-hour or more, then get on the bike for over an hour.

It was exhilarating.

In 2013 (just a few months after The Streak's last day), I entered my first century—a ride that went one hundred miles. I didn't win. Hell, I didn't even come close. But that feeling of getting up in the saddle and driving up a hill, concentrating on a flat area and pushing for miles, was something I had not felt in a long time. It was as if a long-lost friend, who had been wandering in the desert for years, had returned with the same smile and fearlessness he had the last time we'd been together.

PRE

When I worked for Nike in the fall of 1973, there was a memo that went around to all of Nike's stores, stating we needed to host a running clinic. I was still in college at the time and running the company's Garden Grove store, so hosting a clinic while having to accomplish all my other duties was a bit of a challenge. What made the crowd build, however, was when the guys from Nike called to tell me they would be providing some speakers who might attract attention: Steve Prefontaine and his coach, Bill Bowerman. Steve requested to run with a high school team, so I contacted the coaches at Foothill High School to see if they were interested. Running with Steve, less than a year after his US 5K title and his fourth place finish at the Munich Olympics, and having Coach Bowerman show up at their school to speak, let's just say, was something they were not against.

A few weeks later, Steve flew down and stayed the night at my apartment in Fullerton (we had known each other for a few years, so I didn't experience the state of shock most people went into the first time they caught a glance of him). I didn't tell any of my roommates he was coming into town, so when the guys walked into our living room and saw Steve and me sitting on the couch, laughing and swapping stories, it was as close to a religious experience as they'd ever have.

Later that afternoon, Steve and I went over to Foothill High School, where we met with the cross country team and went for a five-mile run. When we got back to campus, Steve and I ran through the gates of the school to the track together, where he told me he wanted to jog a lap or two easy. There was a football practice going on at the time, and when they noticed who was circling their field, practice came to a dead stop. After about twenty seconds of silence, the kids began shouting, "Go Pre," followed by cheers and irrepressible clapping. By the time Steve finished his run, it seemed that every member of the cross country team was at the finish line, waiting to shake his hand or get an autograph. With the start of school still a few weeks away, no one on the team had any notebooks for Steve to sign, so they began forging through trash cans in search of something for Steve to sign. He stayed until everyone who had wanted to shake his hand, get an autograph, or say hello got their turn. The smiles on faces and tears in the eyes of young kids who met Steve that day is something I don't believe anyone there could ever forget.

The next day, our clinic at Long Beach State included a workout from Steve. While Steve ran his 3x1 mile workout solo and clinic goers looked on, Coach Bowerman stood at the starting line, taking splits and discussing with the thirty or so coaches and athletes where this workout fit in their training. Afterwards, we moved into some classrooms as the clinic continued.

Steve had a girl traveling with him, whose name I unfortunately can't remember. When Pre had signed all those autographs, I asked her if this was something he had to deal with all the time. She told me this was a normal occurrence. Each day in Eugene, Steve would receive boxes and boxes of mail from people across the country. Most of the boxes had no delivery address.

They were just addressed "Pre. Eugene, OR."

He was like Santa Claus.

Steve and I finishing our run together at Foothill High School

JULY 23, 2013

Each morning after I get out of bed, I walk in the pitch dark from Debi's and my bedroom, past the kids' rooms, to a long hallway that connects one side of the house to the other. During this early morning walk to the living room, I pass a picture of Steve and me running across the campus at Foothill High School. I also walk past a cabinet that holds a picture of Mom and Dad on their wedding day, along with one of Dad's hats that he wore at the butcher shop, and pictures of our dogs, Clancy and Buckets.

Halfway through the hall there is a piano just a few feet from the picture of Steve and me. It's the piano the kids used to take lessons with when they were younger, and on its top sits a lifetime of memories. Pictures of my daughter's dance recitals, the boys on picture day when they played soccer, and photos of Debi's parents.

That morning stroll down memory lane was something I had done for nearly twenty years in our house in Lancaster, and in all the other places I'd called home since 1968. It was a part of my routine no matter if I felt great, average, or horrible. It was what I did on the days when history was being made all over the world, when people on other coasts were already up and moving, and most people in Lancaster were still sleeping. The run I'd take each day after my hallway stroll didn't define me as a person, but rather served as friend who joined me on a lifetime of memories, who was involved in every major part of my life.

On The Streak's final day, a typical summer day in the Antelope Valley in which the air was dry and the concrete was hot before the sun even rose, the talk amongst everyone who joined me (nearly 250 showed up, some of whom I had never met) wasn't about the miles, or the races, or the injuries, or the blood, or the kidney stones, or the boot—but about what *they* had experienced and learned from my journey of over 16,000 days. I found this humbling, but I also found it surprising. I found it surprising because I didn't think I did much out of the ordinary to keep The Streak alive. Other people may have found things like the boot or my hospital runs crazy, but I saw it as doing something I enjoyed. The Streak provided me with excitement and instilled in me the tools that made me the person, coach, husband, and father I am today.

I was, and still am, someone who considers himself a lucky guy. I found something I loved to do, I found a job that allowed me to do it, and I had a support team around me that continually encouraged me to do what I needed to do to pursue my goals. It didn't matter if those goals involved the team I was attempting to build or a run I was about to go on. Along with lucky, I also see myself as committed. And not just committed when I feel like it. I was blessed enough to learn the skills to remain committed all the time. When you set out to accomplish something—whether it's making the varsity team, trying to lose weight, or attempting to better yourself—you can't just be committed one day and take the next day off. Greatness takes an everyday commitment of work, will, and love. If you want to do something extraordinary, it will be impossible to achieve if it only matters a little. Those who do remarkable things are borderline obsessed with being remarkable and are willing to fully invest themselves in whatever it is they need to do.

There is nothing, I repeat, there is *nothing* wrong with pouring all you are into something because you have a goal. It does not make you odd or strange. It makes you driven. It makes you someone who has a plan and who is willing to adjust their life to fulfill their dream. If someone tells you that you don't need to try as hard, or that what you are doing is not *that* important—they probably lack drive and have no goals.

There is no shame in being committed to your dream and doing what it takes to achieve it.

But commitment—whether it be for two consecutive weeks, four straight years, or forty-five years—is hard.

What made my commitment easier wasn't talent, but rather how I used the skills I learned during my journey. I was able to take in the lessons about toughness that were taught to me by my parents and re-emphasized by Coach Kallem. I learned how to be the best version of myself from Laszlo. I learned when to eliminate excuses and when to take risks, which led to winning the National Championships at Fullerton. I found how out important relationships were from Debi, my kids, and James. And I discovered that even when you spend over forty years doing something, it's okay to walk away if it's in the best interest of your health and your family. It was in these experiences that the impossible became possible and the difficult became doable. It was in that space between decision and action where I found who I was, where I wanted to go, and how much I was willing to hurt to get there.

How did I feel on the final day of The Streak? Honestly, I felt relieved. Relieved I had made it through the run since so many in the days, weeks, and months leading up to it had been such a challenge to get through. And relieved I had ended The Streak the way I'd wanted to. It was on my terms and although it was an incredible challenge to get to and through that 16,436th day, to have experienced what I'd experienced and learned what I did—I wouldn't have changed a thing.

I hope that while reading this book, you have been able to reflect on whatever it is you want to achieve in life, and that you can use some of my lessons to help you get to where you want. Even if you are only able to walk away with one sentence that affected you, one question that allowed you to reflect on your personal journey, or one grain of insight into yourself, then you are closer to achieving your goals than you were before you began reading this. That's not a bad position to be in no matter where you are in your life.

As for me, I continue to ride my bike nearly each day, and I've recently taken up swimming. I retired from coaching in 2017, and then from teaching in 2018. Debi also completed her teaching career as of summer, 2018. Our kids and grandkids are spread across Southern California and other portions of the country, so Debi and I are looking forward to our transition from full-time to completely retired and spending more time with kids and grandkids. And although nothing can replace the feeling of getting up hours before the sun to head out the door on my run, I'm at peace knowing I gained so much more than I had ever dreamed. Now, when I get up to start my day, I may bike, I might swim. (Hell, I may take the day off altogether.) But just knowing there is a challenge out there each day, where I get the opportunity to push myself and see what I can do, no matter the activity, makes my heart soar.

You might even say, it races.

QUESTIONS FOR YOU AND YOUR TEAM

We have made the effort in this book to present an opportunity for you to reflect on your own journey. As much as we hope you enjoyed the lessons and stories, we hope you'll truly examine your own life and decide where you want to go. Whether you are a high school runner, a collegiate football player, an ultra-marathoner, or someone with a nine to five job who doesn't work out, we hope these questions assist you, your team, or both, in identifying areas for needed growth, and places in which you are already strong, as well as heightening your awareness of the path you are currently on.

QUESTIONS FROM PART I
(FOCUS AREA: TOUGHNESS)

1. How do you define "toughness"? _____

   _____

   _____

   _____

   _____

   _____

   _____

   _____

   _____

2. Describe the culture within your organization or team: ___

   _____

   _____

   _____

   _____

   _____

   _____

   _____

3. Can you name the core values of your organization or team?

   _____

   _____

   _____

   _____

   _____

   _____

4. Do the people with whom you surround yourself help you believe in yourself and make you want to become the best you can be? _____

_____

_____

_____

_____

_____

_____

_____

5. If you don't have those people in your social network, what will you do to change it? _____

_____

_____

_____

_____

_____

_____

_____

6. What do you do to make others believe in you? _____

_____

_____

_____

_____

_____

_____

7. Describe what you do to train your mind. How much time do you allocate to it each day? _____

    _____

    _____

    _____

    _____

    _____

    _____

8. Would you consider yourself a risk taker? If so, what makes you think so? If you aren't, what are the things that hinder your ability to "go for it"? _____

    _____

    _____

    _____

    _____

    _____

    _____

9. If toughness is about decision, what choice can you make right now that will allow you to become tougher? _____

    _____

    _____

    _____

    _____

    _____

    _____

QUESTIONS FROM PART II
(FOCUS AREA: BECOMING THE
BEST VERSION OF YOURSELF)

1. Do you keep a journal for your workouts or personal thoughts? If yes, why and if no, why not? _____

   _____

   _____

   _____

   _____

   _____

2. How often do you rely on excuses and what is the scenario (sports, school, work) in which you use them the most? ___

   _____

   _____

   _____

   _____

   _____

   _____

3. When excuses begin to appear in your vocabulary, is it for legitimate reasons or because you are trying to avoid something? _____

   _____

   _____

   _____

   _____

   _____

4. Have there ever been times in your life when you made the clear decision to eliminate excuses to succeed? If so, what specifically did you do and how did the results make you feel?

_____

_____

_____

_____

_____

_____

_____

5. What systems have you established with yourself and/or your team to ensure you are focusing on the process and not the outcome? _____

_____

_____

_____

_____

_____

_____

6. How important do you believe consistency is toward success?

_____

_____

_____

_____

_____

_____

_____

7. What decisions do you make that prevent you from being consistent? _____

_____

_____

_____

_____

_____

8. Are you proud of the decisions you make when you are under stress? If you aren't, what can you commit to, right now, in order to make the best decisions for yourself and the people around you? _____

_____

_____

_____

_____

_____

QUESTIONS FROM PART III
(FOCUS AREA: EMBRACING OPPORTUNITY)

1. Has there ever been a time when someone challenged you to do something that, even though you may have not been in the best emotional, mental, or physical place, made you better after it was over?_____

_____

_____

_____

_____

_____

2. Was there a time in your life where you basked too much in your own successes and stopped persevering? _____

_____

_____

_____

_____

_____

3. When your ego begins to overtake reality, how does that affect your next challenge? _____

_____

_____

_____

_____

4. When you examine your performances, do you tend to judge them or observe them? _____

_____

_____

_____

_____

5. Knowing that observing your performance helps you more than judging it, what can you do in the future to be less hypercritical about negative results? _____

_____

_____

_____

_____

_____

QUESTIONS FROM PART IV
(FOCUS AREA: ACCOUNTABILITY)

What do you do specifically, on a daily basis, to hold yourself and/or your team accountable for what needs to get done?

1. _____

_____

_____

_____

2. Describe a time when someone to whom you made a commitment did not hold up their end of the bargain. What did you do to hold that person accountable? If you didn't, what stopped you from doing so? _____

_____

_____

_____

_____

3. What are the three things that matter the most in your organization or team? _____

_____

_____

_____

4. What are the three things that matter the most in your life?

_____

_____

_____

_____

5. After responding to the two previous questions, does anything stand out to you? Are the things that matter to you and those that matter to your organization on two different ends of the spectrum, or are they similar? What do you think this says about what is important to you and what is important to them?

_____

_____

_____

_____

6. What unique things do you do to motivate yourself and/or your team? _____

_____

_____

_____

7. When you fail to accomplish a goal, what do you do to help yourself move on to the next challenge? _____

_____

_____

_____

8. Failure is something everyone deals with. It's a part of life. However, successful people use failure as an opportunity to examine themselves and improve. What commitments can you make right now that will allow you to use failure as a tool to succeed, rather than an obstacle that stops you from moving forward? _____

_____

_____

_____

9. If you are a part of a large group, especially if you are that group's leader, do you make the effort to learn all of its aspects? If you don't, what can you do to have a greater understanding of how each facet of the group works together? _____

_____

_____

_____

_____

QUESTIONS FROM PART V
(FOCUS AREA: RELATIONSHIPS)

1. Which relationships in your life matter most? _____

_____

_____

_____

_____

2. Of the relationships you just mentioned, what is it about them that makes them so important to you? _____

_____

_____

_____

_____

3. Is there something you do each day that is just for you?___

_____

_____

_____

_____

4. If you don't do anything for yourself, how can you adjust your schedule to give yourself thirty minutes of private time a day?

_____

_____

_____

_____

5. When you travel, do you continue to work out? If you don't, what can you do to create more time when you are on the road? _____

_____

_____

_____

_____

6. Have there been situations, whether in life or in training, in which you feel sorry for yourself and play the victim? If so, what was the reaction of people around you when you did?

_____

_____

_____

_____

7. Do you have a support team? If so, who are they and what do they do to help you? _____

_____

_____

_____

_____

8. If you don't have a support team, what things in your life need support and who can you ask to help? _____

_____

_____

_____

_____

QUESTIONS FROM PART VI
(FOCUS AREA: CHANGE)

1. Are you going through notable changes in your life right now? If you are, what are those changes and how are you dealing with them? _____

_____

_____

_____

_____

2. Do you consider yourself someone who is available? ____

_____

_____

_____

_____

3. When change happens in your life, how well do you adapt to it? Do you get in your own way, or do you just allow it to happen and adjust accordingly? _____

_____

_____

_____

4. What prevents you from adapting positively to changes that are out of your control? _____

_____

_____

_____

_____

5. Is there someone whose determination has inspired you? How did they do it? _____

_____

_____

_____

_____

_____

_____

6. How have you dealt with traumatic events in your life, whether it be the death of a family member, the loss of a job, or something much graver? If you didn't handle it well, what could you have done better to deal with it? _____

_____

_____

_____

_____

_____

_____

_____

_____

_____

QUESTIONS FROM PART VII
(TOPIC: KNOWING WHEN TO WALK AWAY)

1. Nearly all successful people have a morning or evening routine that allows them to either get their day started in the right direction or presents an opportunity to reflect on their day. Do you have a routine, either in the morning or evening, that prepares you to start the day on the right track? If you don't, why don't you have one? _____

   _____

   _____

   _____

   _____

2. Is there a healthy activity you do each day? If not, what would you like to do and what adjustments can you make in your current routine to make it something you do each day, if only for a few minutes? _____

   _____

   _____

   _____

3. When have you had to walk away from something you enjoyed doing? Was that decision easy or difficult— and why? _____

   _____

   _____

   _____

   _____

   _____

4. When you deal with repetitive failure, do you reflect on past successes, or do you try to keep your eyes ahead on the goal at hand? _____

_____

_____

_____

_____

_____

_____

_____

_____

_____

_____

ABOUT THE AUTHORS

Mark Covert

Mark Covert retired in 2017 after twenty-eight years as the head men's and women's cross country and track and field coach at Antelope Valley College, located in Lancaster, California. With a coaching career that spans over forty years, Covert coached one of only four Junior World Cross-Country Champions to come from the United States, over thirty California State Community College Champions, and over twenty championship track and cross-country teams.

Mark began competing in cross-country and track in 1966, for Burbank High School in Burbank, California. During his senior year on July 23, 1968, he began his streak of not missing a day of running that would continue for forty-five years. After graduation, Mark attended Los Angeles Valley Community College, where he would go on to become the state's cross-country champion, along with setting National Junior College records in the six-mile and twenty-four-hour relay. He then went on to attend California State University, Fullerton, where in 1970, he became the NCAA Division II National Cross-Country Champion and the school's first Division I All-American. The following year, Mark and his Fullerton teammates would go on to win the NCAA Division II Cross-Country Championship—a team that has been considered by many to be one of the greatest collegiate cross-country teams of all time.

Mark would go on to compete in the 1972 Olympic Trials in the Marathon, finishing seventh. While doing so, he became the first person to compete in Nike "waffle" racing shoes, and later operated one of Nike's first stores, The Athletic Department. He was the first person named to Nike's Hall of Fame.

Mark is a member of the Mount Sac Cross-Country Hall of Fame, where he remains the only person enshrined as both an athlete and a coach. He also has been inducted to the Los Angeles Valley College Athletic Hall of Fame and the California State University Fullerton Athletics Hall of Fame, and is a founding member of the NCAA Division II Cross-Country Hall of Fame. Mark's success led to Fullerton's Cross-Country team naming their annual home meet after him, known as "The Covert Classic."

After forty-five years of running without taking a day off, Mark ended his running streak in 2013, with several hundred people from across the country gathering at Antelope Valley College to participate in his last run. During his running career, he completed over 163,000 miles (149,000 of those miles run during The Streak) and ran for 16,436 consecutive days, while overcoming broken feet, surgery, seven different stress fractures, and multiple hospitalizations. Mark's story has been featured on ABC Nightly News, The Today Show, and other television and print presses across the world, including Runner's World, CNN, ESPN, and the L.A. Times.

Chris Covert

Chris Covert is Mark's son and the Owner and CEO of Peak Performance Consulting, LLC., a Mental Conditioning & Sports Psychology firm based in Charleston, South Carolina. He has worked with NCAA Individual and Team Champions in football, track and field, and baseball.

A former captain of the Cal State Fullerton Cross Country team, Chris was the former head women's track and cross country coach at Southern Connecticut State University. During his four-year tenure, Chris was named either a Conference or Regional Coach of the Year on nine separate occasions, winning five Conference Championships and working with over thirty NCAA Division II All-Americans. In 2008, he became the youngest coach in NCAA Track and Field history to be named a Regional Coach of the Year, at twenty-five years old. Chris also worked as the Secretary for the United States Track and Cross Country Coaches Association of America from 2009 until 2011. Chris has a bachelor's degree from Cal State Fullerton in kinesiology and a master's degrees in sports psychology and exercise science from Southern Connecticut State University.

Chris has consulted for non-profits, businesses, and political campaigns (working in races spanning from presidential campaigns to municipal races). He has also been a featured speaker for businesses, teams, and universities across the country, covering areas such as organizational management, culture creation, and self-awareness.